A dose of advice for maximizing your retirement

# Prescription for a Happy Retirement

## How to Flourish, not Flounder

**James D. Bash, DO, MPH**

Website: www.rxforahappyretirement.com
Published by JKK Publishing
ISBN: 978-0-692-94276-5
Library of Congress Control Number: 2017953517

Editor: Tyler R. Tichelaar, Superior Book Productions
Cover Design and Interior Book Layout: Larry Alexander,
Superior Book Productions
Author Photo: Scot Fure
Every attempt has been made to source all quotes properly.
Printed in the United States of America
First Edition
2 4 6 8 10 12

To my mother, Joycelynn, who taught me empathy and humor.
My father, Theodore, whose kind and gentle nature influenced me
beyond measure.
My two brothers, Ted and Bob, for their guidance and availability.
My wife, Kathy, and daughter, Katy, for who they are.
And last, but not least, my many patients from whom I sought
and received wisdom.
To these people I will be eternally grateful.

# Acknowledgments

I WOULD LIKE to thank Tyler R. Tichelaar for reading the original manuscript, making beneficial suggestions, and editing. It has been a great experience to work on this project with such an understanding and supportive person. Tyler is extremely gifted at what he does and easy to work with.

I would also like to thank Larry Alexander for doing the layout work and cover. His creative abilities are remarkable, and these skills were of great value in the design and structure of the book.

These two gentlemen went way above and beyond my expectations, and they made what was initially just a pipe dream become a reality. It was a blessing that, while living in a land of iron and copper, I was fortunate enough to find gold.

# Contents

# A Note to the Reader

THERE ARE SIX stages that retirees go through after retiring, just as there are five stages to the grieving process after the loss of a loved one. The third stage of retirement, referred to as the disenchanted/disillusioned stage, and these terms will be used interchangeably throughout the book. It is a time when retirees can feel sad and disappointed. The duration and the intensity of the sadness can vary with the individual retiree. This disillusioned stage most likely serves the purpose of goading retirees to move on and make changes in their lives. The sadness and disappointment associated with retirement are uncomfortable feelings, so most healthy retirees will want to return to a state of happiness or equilibrium. To do that, they will need to figure out for themselves what changes are required. Overall, the disillusioned stage can be a good thing because it pushes retirees to move on with their lives and to adjust. Ideally, retirees will move through the disillusioned stage without consequence so that it has little or no effect on the quality of their lives.

Unfortunately, most retirees don't recognize that the disillusionment they are feeling is trying to tell them some form of change is necessary. They don't take the needed action, whether it be acceptance or the replacement of some of the things that work provided. Under these circumstances, they remain disillusioned for months or even years. The sadness can be perpetuated by feelings of loss of self-esteem, of purpose, of identity, and of relevance. Over time, these feelings will affect the quality of the retirees' lives. They may be unhappy and dissatisfied with the way their lives are going, and that shows up in their behaviors and relationships. They may be more irritable, less attentive, and unmotivated. The disillusioned stage, which started out as good thing, has become prolonged and no longer useful.

This prolonged disillusionment, which is negatively affecting the retiree's life, I call Post-Work Melancholy Syndrome (PMS). If the disillusioned stage is inducing the retiree to change and the appropriate actions are being taken, it is a good thing—even if the process takes several months or even a few years. The problem occurs when the necessary actions are not taken and this sadness goes unaddressed, resulting in a lower quality of life. A happy retirement is based on a good attitude, and it is impossible to have a good attitude if a retiree is suffering from PMS. The premise of this book is to prevent or eliminate the prolonged disillusionment and allow the attitude to improve. Prolonged disillusionment and PMS are used interchangeably in the book.

Although there may be an overlap of some symptoms, the PMS referred to in this book is not at all related to the commonly known Premenstrual Syndrome. The term Post-Work Melancholy Syndrome (PMS) was invented by me. I chose to use PMS because I thought it would be entertaining, easy to remember, and add a little humor to an overall serious subject. It is not meant to be derogatory or offensive, and if offense is taken, I sincerely apologize.

It is possible that a retiree's mood may progress to depression. The treatment of depression is beyond the scope of this text. If a person reading this book is having symptoms of depression, medical attention is recommended.

℞

# Introduction

THE CHANCES ARE good that you'll retire from your job. Baby boomers are arriving at retirement age in increasing numbers, and your retirement may be just over the horizon. You probably haven't given your retirement much thought, other than the financial aspect of it and what you may have observed with retired friends and relatives. You may think your retirement is a long way off or that it will be an easy and natural adjustment. In an ideal world, we could work at a job we enjoy right up until the time we meet our demise, but for most of us, that isn't likely. A small fraction of people will be able to work beyond their recommended retirement age, but for most of us, retirement comes upon us quickly, and it is a major and often unsettling life change. Most people underestimate the magnitude of that change. I know I did.

Retirement is a time when you can finally live the life you were destined to live. You can design your ideal life and then put it into practice. At the same time, I've seen a lot of people who have not adjusted well to it. It's up to you to make the retirement years the best years ever. That's what this book is intended to help you do.

Oddly, most books on retirement don't address ways of dealing with this very important time in a person's life. The majority of books focus on retirement's financial aspects. Many are written by people who may be decades away from retiring. Certainly, money is important, but money is only part of it. It's much better to learn about retirement and its potential pitfalls from someone who has lived it and continues to live it. This book comes from the heart. It's based on my personal experiences and many years of study. While practicing medicine, I saw people who aged well and went through many of life's transitions with ease. I also saw plenty of the opposite—people unprepared for the big changes. They had no idea what to expect or how to prepare for changes. Many had no guidance or access to resources to help with the process.

Because I have experienced retirement, I have come to some very beneficial conclusions, and now I want to share them with you. In the years that I have been retired, I have learned a lot about myself and about life. Certainly, much worse things can happen to a person than retirement, but when it happens to you, it can be quite a shock. In my opinion, living the principles shared in this book is the best way to have a fulfilling retirement. In my case, it is the only way. The ideas found in this book are not new. These basic recommendations have stood the test of time. When I retired, I was unaware of the need to follow these principles, and I suspect you are too. Keep reading to find out what these common-sense principles are.

Retirement may be the biggest change we must deal with in life. Change often brings on stress, and retirement coincides with other major life changes—aging, decreased energy levels, a change in status and family roles, and possibly major changes in income. These changes are not to be taken lightly. No matter who you are or what your situation is, there will be an adjustment phase. You may go through a grieving period lasting weeks or even longer. It is referred to as the "disenchantment/disillusionment" phase and is one of the stages of retirement. It is normal because you're acclimating to a whole new way of life. You may become disillusioned and have feelings of "Whoops! I made a mistake." It's normal to have these feelings after you retire. You've made a major change in your life that can't be ignored or put on the back burner.

A period of grieving is expected when you retire. However, a fairly large percentage of people fail to adjust and move beyond the disenchantment phase. Instead, they become sad and melancholy for an extended period. They may even continue to spiral down and become depressed. I'm sure we all know people who fit this description. We may even feel this way ourselves.

This book is designed to help you recognize and prevent that downward spiral into melancholy, or if you're already experiencing it, teach you how not to let it affect your quality of life. For me, the most enjoyable part of being a physician was helping people overcome difficult times in their lives. I want to be able to do the same with this book. Its ideas and recommendations have helped me enjoy a meaningful retirement, and they can work for you.

I've learned from experience that we can be happy with this stage of life if we can accept that we don't need more than our basic needs to be satisfied. Then we can concentrate all our energies on improving our attitudes. This, of course, isn't easy. We have spent years living a certain way, so we have formed many beliefs that have served us well while working and raising a family. We also have values and assumptions that were instilled in us from childhood. These beliefs and values, however, may no longer be beneficial at this stage in life. For example, if you believe you must be gainfully employed in order be of value, then you're unlikely to be content in retirement. But we can't change our beliefs with a snap of our fingers. Rather, we need to be constantly aware of our beliefs and work slowly and steadily on changing them. Our attitudes are dynamic and always changing because our life circumstances are constantly changing.

At any moment, due to a change in circumstances, our attitudes can take a nosedive. That is why we have to take responsibility for our attitudes. We can't let ourselves be buffeted by outside events. We can't control our circumstances, but we can control our attitudes about them. We need to set the stage so that a good attitude can develop and be maintained. Clearing the debris from our minds is necessary for developing and maintaining a good attitude.

There's been a lot of discussion that sixty is the new forty, and that people should plan to work well beyond normal retirement age. I couldn't disagree more. The average retirement age in this country is sixty-three, and only about a third of people sixty-five and older are still employed. We see people like Warren Buffet and others working well into their eighties, but when you own your own business, provided you have the financial means, you can retire when you want. Furthermore, times have changed and jobs have evolved; most people no longer have the opportunity to work at the same job for thirty or more years.

When to retire may not be your choice; the decision may be the organization's or someone else's to make. Health or family issues may require you to retire at an unexpected time. Most people end up retiring at a younger age than they expected. The odds are that it won't happen exactly as you anticipate.

## *I Was Unprepared for Retirement*

When I started out in my career as a doctor, I never thought that I would retire in my fifties. I assumed my career would be long and enjoyable. After ten years of being on call and putting in all-consuming hours, however, I began to realize this was not the life I wanted for many more years. That realization happens to all of us, but at different times. At a certain point in our working lives, we think about making a career change or about leaving work entirely, and that's what happened to me. I started to think about my alternatives, and I began reading about and studying retirement, both the financial and emotional sides. I continued to work long days, weekends, and holidays for fifteen more years, all the while reading, studying, and planning for my eventual retirement.

But even though I put in all that preparation, I was woefully unprepared when the day came. I was under the impression that retirement would take care of itself and there would be little effort required. Boy, was I wrong. I had read books and talked to people about retirement, but it wasn't what I had imagined. If you want a retired life where you just float around without purpose, little effort is needed. But I knew that I wanted more out of life, so I had to do the required work to achieve it.

## *Stages of Adjustment to Retirement*

The PMS I talk about in this book is not the same PMS that women of reproductive age experience. Post-Work Melancholy Syndrome is the name I've given to the sadness and emptiness that often accompanies retirement. I call it a syndrome because it is marked by sadness, but it can be associated with an array of other problems. It can manifest as irritability or mood swings, and it can lead to more serious problems, like depression and anxiety.

It is helpful to know that a retired person goes through six stages of adjustment that are very similar to the stages of grief we experience when we suffer a significant loss. The stages are:

1.  preretirement
2.  retirement
3.  disenchantment/disillusionment
4.  reorientation
5.  retirement routine
6.  termination of retirement

Most of us go through all these stages once we retire, but the order in which we experience them and how much time we spend in each stage may vary. It is not a concern if someone is progressing through the stages and appears to be adapting to the transition. The problem arises when someone gets stuck in the disenchanted stage or becomes melancholic and can't get out. This disenchanted feeling, if prolonged, can lead to sadness, hopelessness, and a downward spiral in your emotional state. Such a situation can be very confusing to the retired person and his or her family. None of them understand what's happening, so they aren't sure what to do about the problem.

It's common to become disillusioned with retirement; I know because I've gone through that phase and so have many other people I've known. However, disillusionment can be a positive experience, and it can lead to personal growth. It did for me, and the same can happen for you.

One problem we face is our expectations about retirement. We're told retirement is supposed to be one of the most enjoyable times of our lives, and yet the retired person may find it's just the opposite. We're uncomfortable talking to family members and friends about our disenchantment. It's hard to admit that retirement feels like a mistake. Not many people can relate to these feelings if they haven't gone through retirement. If you do admit to these feelings, you might be told that you're lucky to be retired, and you should get a hobby and quit complaining.

The inability to talk effectively to others and gain their understanding makes it even more difficult to escape disillusionment. The retiree may be functioning fine on the surface, but he or she continues to feel sad and unfulfilled. Getting caught in this disenchanted stage or becoming sad is what I mean by the melancholy of retire-

viii James D. Bash, DO, MPH

ment. You're stuck and don't know what to do or whom to turn to.

The ideas and recommendations in this book can drastically reduce, in duration and severity, your disillusionment and negative feelings about retirement. The prescription for a happier retirement that this book offers you will help you prevent PMS, but the stage of disenchantment can't be eliminated. In fact, I wouldn't want that to happen because it's a great chance for personal growth and self-discovery. While a prolonged period of disenchantment can lead to sadness or melancholy, and eventually to depression, a short period of disenchantment can gradually evolve into a much happier state of mind. I know this from my own experience. If we recognize that disenchantment is a normal phase of retirement, then we can take steps to reduce its length and intensity and use it to transform how we view and use retirement.

## *A Time of Great Growth and Learning*

When viewed from the proper perspective, retirement can be an extremely beneficial time of life, a time of great growth and learning. The stages we experience as a result of transitioning out of the work world cannot be fully prevented. The transition is a process we all must go through in order to develop a new beginning. But it doesn't have to be traumatic and debilitating.

Retirement gets a bad rap in many ways. People often view it as "the last frontier" before we move on to never-never land—the end of the rope, being put out to pasture, and becoming irrelevant to society. If it is the last frontier, why waste it living in the past or thinking about what might have been? I strongly feel retirement can be the most productive time of our lives. It's a time when we take better care of ourselves both mentally and physically, and when we can actually make the biggest contribution to society. We have the opportunity to set an example for the younger generations. After all, what could be better for society than a person who is happy, vibrant, fulfilled, and mentally healthy?

Retirement gives us the freedom to do the things that bring us the most joy. It's a time when we can remove the shackles of other people's expectations and live life on our terms. When you're feeling good about life and yourself, you're more apt to share and be generous with others. It's also a time when you can shed the negativity in your life. In the work world, we can't choose our workmates and colleagues. If someone is annoying or negative in our retirement, we can choose to have that person be less involved in our lives.

Retirement is a gift to be enjoyed, not to be wasted. It's not a time to lie fallow, although initially that may be of some benefit. Retirement is a time to learn about life in general and also about ourselves. When used properly, this time will give us insight into what makes us tick.

Retirement is not the end of our lives. It's truly a new beginning.

To help you on this journey, I will address major issues related to why people can have trouble with being retired and how to have a happy retirement. The material is covered in ten chapters. Here is a brief overview of each one:

### Chapter One: How I Learned to Love Retirement

Most people underestimate the magnitude of the changes brought about by retirement. I know I did. In this chapter, I talk about my initial disillusionment with retirement, what I learned from that experience, and how you can learn from my experience to create a good life for yourself in retirement.

### Chapter Two: The Foundations of PMS

Leaving the work environment can cause melancholy, low self-esteem, and a sense of worthlessness. If not recognized and dealt with, these feelings can lead to depression and major physical health problems. In this chapter, I look at some of the reasons why people flounder during retirement and what you can do to address the causes of your dissatisfaction.

### Chapter Three: Anticipate and Plan for Retirement While You're Still Working

The time when you retire may be completely out of your hands; there's a much greater chance that you'll retire before your set retirement age than not. That's why it's so important to plan for your retirement well in advance, both financially and emotionally. Being aware of the potential problems you may encounter before you retire and planning for how to address them is the key to a successful retirement.

### Chapter Four: Understand the Difference Between Needs and Wants

The more conditions you establish for your happiness, the harder it will be to realize success in retirement. That's why it's so important to think about what you'll need to be happy. Better yet, figure out what you *don't* need to have a successful retirement.

### Chapter Five: Build Your Identity and Self-Esteem on Solid Ground

In retirement, you can finally take off all the masks you've been wearing and be who you really are. If you don't know who you are, there's no better time to find out. Some may find this opportunity intimidating, but it's also freeing. Up until now, your identity was probably largely defined by work, but now it's time to let go of that identity and find a better one. Retirement is a time when we can learn about ourselves and become who we were meant to be—in other words, living authentically with an identity built on solid ground.

### Chapter Six: Your Mind Creates Reality

All of life should be savored and enjoyed, even the trials and difficulties. Most of the bad events that happen to us in life are made worse and last longer because of our reactions to them. In this chapter, I'll show you how to optimize your thinking. Becoming more aware of our self-sabotaging tendencies can make a big difference in the way we feel about ourselves. Just thinking positive thoughts is not enough. If that were the case, everyone would be happy and well-adjusted. In this chapter, we'll look at how we can use our minds in beneficial ways rather than being used by them.

### Chapter Seven: A Few Core Principles for Emotional Health

To develop and maintain a good attitude and emotional health, you have to construct a strong foundation based on a few core principles. In this chapter, I will look at the principles, behaviors, and actions that will lead to emotional health at this crucial time in your life.

### Chapter Eight: Don't Neglect Your Physical Health

Nearly 70 percent of Americans are overweight and more than one third are considered obese. A good portion drink alcohol regularly and many imbibe excessively. Most people don't exercise enough, and the majority get no beneficial exercise at all. Many people are forced to retire because of health problems and disabilities. We may be living longer, but that doesn't mean we're living healthier. In this chapter, we'll look at the importance of maintaining good physical health before and during retirement.

### Chapter Nine: Plan for Lifelong Financial Health

It's hard to enjoy your retirement if you're constantly worried about money. Your fiscal health is as important as your physical health; in some cases, it's more important. In this chapter, I'll show you how to save for retirement and give you tips on how to live well but frugally.

### Chapter Ten: Engage in Lifelong Activity and Learning

Entertaining ourselves is better than being entertained. Being actively involved in some activity you enjoy can be satisfying and productive. If I sit and watch TV, I'll feel empty and tired. But if I take a walk or work on a project, in most cases, I'll feel invigorated. Since I've retired and had unstructured time, I've noticed that I feel more creative. It's very difficult to be creative when you're going a million miles an hour at work. The greater your free time, the more your potential for creativity grows, and you can develop it in areas you never thought possible.

*** 

It's so important to move successfully through the disenchantment stage of retirement so you can make the most of your life and enjoy it as much as possible. Most people don't realize what a gift life is until they, a friend, or a loved one has a life-changing event. Some people don't slow down until they have a heart attack or get some dreaded disease like cancer. In her book *The Top Five Regrets of the Dying*, Bronnie Ware, a hospice nurse, states that the second biggest regret of dying people was working too hard. It's even purported that Sam Walton said on his deathbed, "I blew it." The prescription offered in these pages is designed to help you value and appreciate life to the fullest in your retirement years.

Before we move on to Chapter One, I want to tell you a story. Mr. Smith (not his real name) was a patient of mine for approximately ten years before he had to be admitted to a nursing home. He'had been a prominent member of the community and was very well-known. He had a college education and ran his own business. His wife was intelligent and attractive, and he had two successful children living in different states. His wife died two years before he was admitted to the nursing home. Mr. Smith had been doing well at home until he started falling and needed more help.

After being admitted to the nursing home, Mr. Smith became depressed, but he told me he was going to try his best to adapt. In about two months, he had adjusted to his new environs. One day, I dropped in to see how he was doing. When I entered his room, he was asleep in the green chair next to his bed.

I looked around the room. On his bedside table were a dish of apple slices that were turning brown and a bowl of rice pudding covered with plastic wrap. On a corner of the table was a container half-full of urine. The part of the room he occupied was about 10 by 10, with a curtain dividing Mr. Smith's space from his roommate's.

When I tapped him on the shoulder, he woke up easily. I listened to his heart and lungs, and then I asked him whether we could have a chat. He happily agreed. He was as sharp mentally as I had ever seen him. I asked him how he was doing.

Without hesitation, he blurted out, "I'm very happy." I must have looked surprised because he then said, "I have all the ingredients for happiness. I have a place to stay for shelter. I have regular food that doesn't taste bad. I have socialization with the staff and visitors. The rest is just an attitude thing."

We talked a while longer, and then I wished Mr. Smith well and left. As I walked out to my car, I wondered whether I would be as capable of the same positive and accepting outlook if I ended up in a nursing home or had similar losses.

I quickly forgot about the incident and never thought about it again until many years had passed and I had been retired for over a year. I was still adjusting to retirement and was questioning why I was not feeling quite as exuberant as I thought I should be feeling. One day, out of the blue, the memory of Mr. Smith came back to me. He had lost just about everything: his home, independence, mobility, spouse, family, business, status, and health. Other than being alive, he had what most people would consider very little to live for. How, then, could Mr. Smith possibly have been happy?

And why was I so unsettled when I had so much more than he had? I still had my health, family, spouse, independence, and enough money. Then it dawned on me. I remembered what Mr. Smith had said near the end of our conversation: "The rest is just an attitude thing." I had all the other basic ingredients, but I needed to work on my attitude.

As I've been going through the stages of retirement, I've understood the magnitude of the change involved. The most important lesson I've learned is that how well or poorly we do in retirement is totally based on our state of mind. I realize now that I'm the one responsible for how well my retirement goes. I can control my thoughts and my feelings, or, if not control them, have a different take on them. I don't have all the answers, but I certainly have a better understanding of what makes for a happy retirement. We need to figure out what's important for ourselves in life and make it happen. No one else can determine what's best for us.

Not every idea or recommendation in this book will be right for you. Everyone's situation is different, so what's important to me in retirement may not be important to you. No one can tell you exactly how to live in retirement. It's up to each one of us to find out what works best and to put it into action. However, what this book can do is to help you eliminate the trial and error that goes along with any type of change. What took me many months to discern is in these pages. Instead of having to figure out what is causing you to feel less enthusiastic about your retirement, you can start right in on making it better. The path has been cleared; all you have to do is follow it and enjoy the vista.

The main way to treat PMS is to work on removing barriers to being happy, which is a lifelong process. This is not something you do once and forget about, but as you become more adept at recognizing these stumbling blocks, it gets easier to remove them. This removal frees up time and energy so you can work on improving your attitude. The goal is not to eliminate problems but to have enough confidence in our abilities to handle them so we feel better about life and can develop and live from our authentic selves. Living authentically and in the present moment can be the closest we ever come to heaven on earth. The prescription referred to in this book is really about writing your own prescription for retirement. In the following pages, you will learn how.

At the end of each chapter, there will be questions and possibly exercises to help you think about the subject matter found in the chapter. Spend two or three minutes on each question formulating your answers. Your answers will help you gain insight into how prepared you are for retirement. If you are already retired, then contemplating the questions and taking action, based on your answers, may greatly enhance your retirement experience.

Now let's begin the journey together.

R̸X

*Chapter One*

# How I Learned to Love Retirement

I WAS BORN in 1955, and I grew up in a small town in Michigan, the middle child with two brothers. My father was a physician and my mother a nurse. My father's practice was upstairs in our home. He was the typical small-town doctor who was always available. He was also the most honest and conscientious person I've ever known. Because his office was in the home and always open, I got a lot of exposure to the medical profession from a very early age.

My brothers and I would sometimes help patients upstairs and to get situated before my father would see them. Sometimes we assisted him with suturing and minor emergency procedures. My mother and father were very devoted to the practice and never turned anyone away. My father took phone calls throughout the night and saw patients Monday through Saturday, for regular hours, and whenever someone showed up at the office after hours. He did hospital work and also made house calls. As a result, he was very much overworked.

When I started college, I wasn't really interested in medicine as a career. I had seen firsthand how much of a time commitment was involved and wasn't sure I wanted the same lifestyle. I found that I enjoyed the sciences, so I was planning on becoming an optometrist because it seemed less time-demanding than being a physician. But while applying to optometry schools, I also applied to medical school. I was accepted first to optometry school, but I remembered my dad telling me not to accept the position until I heard from medical school. When the medical school also accepted me, I felt honored and couldn't turn it down.

After finishing med school and my residency, I settled in a rural area in Michigan where I started a practice with two other physicians. We also did hospital and nursing home work. Our practice was one of the few that took state insurance. I worked eight to fifteen hours a day Monday through Friday, and another five or six hours on Saturdays. The call schedule was one to two nights weekly and one weekend a month, but most of the time it was more often. My practice and responsibility grew very rapidly, and soon the hours became even longer. It eventually got to the point where I was getting up at 4 a.m. and arriving home at 7:30 p.m. or later. Then I had to be up most of the night taking calls. If I could get out of the office for thirty minutes at lunchtime, I took a nap in my car.

### An Unsustainable Lifestyle

When I got into my fifties, I noticed that I couldn't recover as well after being on call all night. It would take me two or three days to recover, and by then, I was on call again. One weekend, I had a kidney stone and went to the ER. I was given pain medication for the discomfort on Saturday morning, but I was on call that weekend. None of my partners were available to cover for me. The pain subsided somewhat and I could work, but it was starting to dawn on me that this type of lifestyle was going to be hard to maintain. My partners and myself, and most likely all rural physicians, have to be available whether we have health or family issues or not. You never can call in sick.

I started to become sleep-deprived and had no life outside of my work. I started to worry that something major would happen to my health. In 2005, my partners and I sold the practice to a hospital and I became an employee. I was still working the same hours, but I was no longer the owner. I had liked medicine, but I was finally beginning to feel burned out. I had had enough of carrying a pager and cell phone so I could be reached at any time. I was partially to blame since I wasn't good at setting boundaries. It was very difficult for me to tell patients I would see them the following week. I always tried to fit them in on the day they called and, like my father, I never turned anyone away.

When I was working on my Master's in Public Health, I did a research project on stress management in the workplace. I had a keen interest in this subject for my personal benefit and that of my patients. I was aware of how excessive stress can negatively affect our lives. The stress I faced in my job was real and could potentially cause health problems.

I started noticing little signs that the stress was catching up to me. I did very little socializing because I usually got up at 4:00 a.m. I developed writer's cramp in my right hand and had to write with my left. I felt tense all the time, always anticipating my pager going off or the phone ringing, which it usually did.

I eventually started to lose my focus, which was frightening to me because I always liked to be on top of everything. I didn't want to be just an average doctor. Here I was telling patients to get enough rest and take care of themselves, but I wasn't following my own advice.

### A Life-Changing Epiphany

I knew that the schedule would eventually ruin my health and possibly other important aspects of my life. My dad developed diabetes when he was forty-eight, and I'm certain it was related to his heavy schedule. I remember him saying that he wished he had retired earlier because by the time he retired, he wasn't healthy enough to do the things he wanted to do. The final straw for me was when my wife had to have major surgery. That event changed my life forever. I then realized how quickly a person's life can be altered and how fragile life really is. I knew then that I didn't want to devote my whole life to my career. I wanted to enjoy the people who meant the most to me, so I came to the conclusion that a major change had to be made. When my contract was up and my daughter was done with high school, I would leave medicine and start anew.

It was by no means an easy decision. I had grown close to many patients during my twenty-three years in this rural practice. One of my partners was like a brother to me. But I had finally had enough.

The timing couldn't have been better for my retirement. My wife wanted to move back to her hometown to be close to her aging parents, and I felt it was time to move on. I had always been good at saving money. We lived frugally and had very little debt. Most of our vacations were spent in my wife's hometown so we could visit with her family. We had enough money to support a decent quality of life.

### Unprepared for the Great Change

You've probably heard that you shouldn't retire *from* something, but rather retire *to* something. I did the former, so I wasn't prepared for the great change I encountered. I went from working my usual day to being unemployed. In fact, my last day of work, I was on call and up all night. It took me several months to learn to live at a different pace. I felt tired but didn't sleep well. Now I had all this time on my hands, but I didn't know exactly what to do with it. It had been indoctrinated in me from a very young age that work was central to one's life; now that belief was in conflict with my new lifestyle.

I felt like a boat drifting on the ocean without a direction or a safe harbor. Having no set schedule or tasks to measure my life by was a new and uncomfortable experience. If I became involved in a project or activity, I felt better, yet the anxiety would return whenever I had too much time on my hands. I knew I didn't want to go back to my old situation, but I wanted to be involved in something that would inspire me and get me excited again.

Instead of being fun and exciting, retirement was a rude awakening. I was happy with my decision to leave work, but I felt as if there was nothing more for me to do in life. It wasn't until I stopped working that I realized I had devoted most of my life to my job. I was lacking competency in other activities and aspects of life.

My wife had her routine around the house and my daughter was in college, but I didn't have anything I was passionate about. That's when I started reading more about retirement to find out how people were able to iron out the bumps. I read about, studied, and observed people who appeared to be doing well in retirement. I even became a certified retirement coach so I could coach myself and enhance my retirement.

What I learned was certainly beneficial, but it didn't alleviate my disillusionment. Most of the recommendations I read were centered on replacing what you had when you were working—the structure, income, status, and feeling of usefulness. I didn't feel that making retirement a continuation of my work life was the best approach for me. I know that work brings many benefits to people's lives and it's a measure of how well we're doing in life, but most of us become too dependent on these attributes of our jobs. What makes us feel useful and successful in life is both relative and subjective. I wanted to become less dependent on those external things. I felt it would be better to understand why we feel we need those things and to try to change the beliefs that perpetuate those feelings.

For me, searching to replace what I had gained from working was just delaying the acceptance of life's unavoidable losses. I thought it would be better to approach this unchartered time of life with less trappings and more freedom. If I desired structure, I could spend my time doing things I wanted to do, and that didn't necessarily result in increased status or financial benefit. I didn't just want to "be busy." I wanted to replace my previous career with something exciting and invigorating—the kind of feeling I had experienced when I first started out as a doctor.

### *The Power of Our Minds to Shape Reality*

Early in retirement, I started reading about how our minds can either help or harm us. The subject is fascinating and enlightening, and it made me realize how powerful our minds are and the problems they can cause if not properly managed. I've concluded that we all have the ability to live good lives and that ability is under our control. Most of what we encounter in life is not under our control, but our reactions to and thoughts about what we encounter *are* in our control. We have the ability to be upbeat about any situation or event that happens to us, or at least the choice to view it in a less negative fashion. If we're able to view retirement as gaining freedom instead of losing our identity, our attitude can improve.

In nature, status or hierarchy is beneficial for obtaining food and a mate. In the human world, status is whatever you define it to be. The acquisition of food is usually not a problem, and most retirees aren't actively seeking a mate. It's possible to develop your own definition of status—being the happiest retired person or the best grandpa or whatever you want it to be. Status is really how you feel about yourself. If you feel good about yourself, the traditional measures of status don't matter. Just making it to retirement is quite a feat.

My work was a pleasure most of the time, but I now realize I couldn't be my true self when I was working. I had to be available even when I wanted to do other things, and I had to agree to things that didn't seem right. I was accountable to too many people and overseers. Administrators, owners, insurance companies, staff, and patients seemed to expect me to be accessible all the time. I was always feeling tense and stressed because I felt the need to please everyone. This is common in the caring professions and often leads to burnout.

It was difficult to show my true feelings; in fact, I wasn't sure what my true feelings were because I had never really delved into them. It's not healthy to be someone you're not; in fact, it requires a lot of energy. When you're younger, you don't notice the strain as much, but when you're older, your energy reserves become drained. I don't think this experience was limited to me; my perception is that it is this way for everyone.

It is common for us not to be our true selves at work. We must follow rules we may not agree with and tolerate workers and clients we may have conflicts with. Over time, this leads to a lack of focus and even cynicism. It's probably not possible to be 100 percent who we really are because we'll always have to deal with other people and circumstances. But the closer we come to our true selves, the better, and retirement offers that opportunity.

### *Learning to Live Authentically*

We are all born with different abilities and talents. Our aspirations and dreams are unique. If our abilities, talents, and dreams are suppressed, we'll be unhappy. Living as authentically as possible should be the ultimate goal in life. And I've come to believe, despite my earlier disillusionment, that retirement affords us that opportunity.

After much reading, studying, and contemplating, I've found that life is much more satisfying when I can call my own shots. There are no rules governing how we're to live in retirement. We get to set the rules. Of course, laws need to be followed, and we all have our responsibilities, but we can design our own lives. Getting the chance finally to create the life you want to live is exciting and energizing, and we can also make a greater contribution to society when we're happy.

I'd be lying if I told you I'm always happy in retirement. But my job isn't to be happy all the time. Rather, it's to make the most of my retirement years. Retirement is a time for self-discovery, which is a lifelong process. What can be better than having the opportunity to get to know yourself and then doing what you find most important in life? Determining what makes you happy and then pursuing it is the best that it gets.

I know I'm a retiree in progress and still learning. I also know it would be impossible to enjoy retirement if I were not applying what I've already learned. It's so important to let go of the baggage we may be carrying, such as resentment, anger, jealousy, and guilt. It's also very important to ease up on the worry and fear of failure. If you are a people pleaser or codependent, now is the time to change. Falling into self-criticism will only play havoc with your life in retirement.

This is the time to be who you really are. Enjoy your uniqueness and share your individual gifts with loved ones and society. Be gracious and approach life as a gift. Just being alive is a gift worth being thankful for. Retirement is a chance to shine in the areas you choose. At this point in life, you've paid your dues. Now you deserve to live the life you desire.

Retirement is your journey and nobody else's. It's up to you to decide what's best for you. You can't please others or rely on people to make you happy; for each of us, happiness is a self-directed project.

## Questions for Reflection

1) What is your story? How did you end up in your occupation?

2) Are you happy in your current situation? Why or why not?

3) How do you view retirement? What are those views based on?

4) Do you know anyone who appears successful in retirement? Why is he or she doing so well?

5) What are your greatest fears about retirement? If you are already retired, are you adjusting well?

6) Do you have any feelings that a change is needed?

℞

Chapter Two
The Foundations of PMS

BEFORE WE GET into how we can change and work on our attitudes, I would like to talk more about why we have such a hard time with retirement.

Retirement can be a major shock to the system. Even though I had read several books about it and tried to prepare myself mentally, I found that it was a much bigger challenge than I had thought. Here is an overview of the major reasons why people flounder during retirement. In the chapters that follow, we'll go into more detail about each of these issues.

### You've Over-Identified with Work

Work has provided value to your life and has allowed you, through its financial benefits, to live the life of your choosing. You have received many benefits from your employment—income, socialization, and a sense of utility, status, and identity. You have also felt a sense of belonging and the feeling of being needed. You've earned the respect, admiration, and trust of your fellow workers. In your job, you may have felt your life had meaning and that you were providing a service to society. You may have had a title and a private office, and you may have been involved in making important decisions. The working environment definitely had benefits, and a lot of emotion, hard work, and time were wrapped up in your career.

For these reasons, giving up the duties you've had in the working world is hard for most people. Having people respect and pay for your time is very gratifying. We certainly don't want to give up this kind of power and authority. But our self-esteem can be too closely tied to this ephemeral power, and we can mistakenly expect it to last forever.

Eventually, we're going to have to give it up. Nothing, including ourselves, lasts forever. And by being so invested in the power of work, we've had to make concessions in our personal lives. We've had to give up our time, and our ability to control our life has been limited.

For most of our life, the tradeoff has been worth it. But as we get older and have fewer obligations, we can most likely reclaim control of our life. Giving up our power at work will allow us to obtain the most priceless power we can ever hope to possess—the power to manage our own time and life. We don't have to be at a certain place at a designated time. We don't have to put up with evaluations and bosses, deadlines and coworkers. We're now our own boss.

This change can be scary for some people and a hard adjustment to make. But you can get the same rewards as you got from working, just on a smaller scale. The most important thing is to gain self-respect outside of your work identity.

Unfortunately, no matter how much we love our jobs and the material and emotional benefits they supply, work can't last forever. You may never get the same type of respect again; you may no longer be referred to as "Doctor" or another professional title. If you've identified too much with your job, the adjustment to retirement will be more difficult.

### Something Seems Missing

Sometimes in retirement, you just don't feel right. You feel like something is missing and your excitement for life isn't as great. With some retirees, this feeling is short-lived, but it becomes a long-term problem for others. It can go unnoticed because your life seems to be going okay, and when you notice the feelings, you may just attribute them to your age. Disenchantment and melancholy are also something that most retirees won't talk about because of embarrassment and fear of failure. Plus, you don't get much sympathy from friends and colleagues who are still working and can't identify with your problem.

Retirees will often say, "I don't know where the time goes; I'm so busy," or "This is the best job I've ever had." But when you look deeper, you find that their time is being filled with uninspiring, passive activities.

When we lose our work-related self-esteem, we have to work on building it up in other areas of our lives. Being a good husband or wife, a good parent, or a respectable citizen and neighbor can all elevate our self-esteem. We also need to accept ourselves for who we are and move along from there.

Yet going through the process of adjusting to retirement can also raise your self-esteem. If done right, it can be the most enjoyable process of your life. It takes time and patience, but when done correctly, it will lead to a much more enjoyable life and a better understanding of yourself.

### Failure to Grow and Learn

The reason some people become melancholic during retirement is because they fail to grow and learn. Some even regress. They live totally passive lives, watching hours of TV, drinking alcohol to excess, or gambling, to name a few of the activities they find to pass the time. These activities provide some pleasure in the short-term, but they can't provide sustainable satisfaction.

Other people stay in neutral, not regressing but not really growing either. They follow the crowd and fill their time with activities like golfing, playing bridge, and entertainment travel. Life isn't exactly what they want, but they're okay with it.

The positive growth group is doing many of the same activities as the neutral growth people, but they're expanding their horizons and learning new things. They're exploring their interests rather than just following the crowd. They're pursuing new skills, playing a new instrument, or learning a new language. By developing their creativity, they're finding more fulfillment in life.

Fulfillment is something we each have to search for and then pursue. Finding a new interest and then developing it can be the most satisfying feeling in retirement. It does take some internal work to determine what you would like to aim for, but it's worth it. Nothing in life is easy, but directing your own life and chasing what you want out of life will be very gratifying. You've waited decades for this chance, so it shouldn't be wasted. It's a journey only you can take—to get to know yourself better.

Whatever your life in retirement is, you get to orchestrate it. The other path—not growing at all or growing in a negative way—will only lead to melancholy and depression, and then to despair. Staying in neutral can be enjoyable, but you'll most likely feel like you're missing something in life. It's like eating only cake and ice cream every day. It tastes good and can keep you alive, but it doesn't provide you with the nutrition you need for a happy, healthy life.

The disenchanted and melancholy feelings are an indication that positive growth is needed. Here is where we can try to understand why we feel the way we do. Then we can work on solutions. We've been working at our jobs so long and hard that we don't even know ourselves and what we want out of life. The job's demands and those of other people have left no time for us to know ourselves.

It's easier just to go with negative or neutral growth and not have to bother with any effort. Yet this will not lead to a satisfying retirement in most cases because you'll always be looking for more. Learning about yourself and what your interests are is well worth the effort and time. The process does not happen overnight, but takes a lifetime.

Asking yourself questions like "Who am I?" and "What can bring meaning to my life?" is a start. Paying attention to your emotional response to events and activities can also help. Any way that you're improving yourself leads to positive growth, such as developing new skills, a new hobby, or socializing more. Even very small gains can add up over time. The gradual and slow changes we make in our lives are what make growth possible and sustainable.

A good question to ask frequently is: "Is the activity I'm doing leading to positive emotional growth?"

### *The Need to Be Busy All the Time*

The hardest part of retirement for me is the feeling that I should be doing something all the time. Not just anything, but using my time to accomplish some important task. I've set a lot of goals in my retirement, so I don't want to waste time on frivolous activities. This feeling is almost a compulsion for me, as my wife and daughter can attest.

I was retired for a while before I became aware of this. It was engrained in me at a very young age not to waste time and to be productive. Not being productive made me feel anxious, so I probably used work to distract me from that anxiety. I was a workaholic as a doctor, and then, I suddenly retired. Overnight, I went from 100 miles an hour to 10 miles an hour with no adjustment period.

I wouldn't recommend this approach to the faint of heart. If work has become your identity, if you've used it to distract yourself from certain emotions and thoughts, it could be very difficult to make a sudden adjustment to a slower lifestyle. It's important to recognize whether this will be a possible issue for you; then you can make changes and adjustments in preparing for retirement. In some cases, leaving the work world is similar to kicking a drug habit or something we've become dependent upon for coping with life.

This need to be busy is the reason a lot of people fail at retirement, at least at first. Some people feel the need to be busy all the time, and when they're no longer busy, the discomfort is immense. Most don't recognize this as a problem until retirement. To be successful at your job, you've had to put in a lot of time and effort. You've gotten recognition and enjoyment, but when it's time to stop, you're ill-prepared. Many of us suffer from perfectionism and are very attached to what we achieve at work. If I had it to do over, I would have tried to take more time off to develop other interests. But I'm also glad I worked hard when I did so that now I can dictate the kind of life I want.

### *Failure to See Melancholy as a Gift*

As I alluded to earlier, the melancholy you may be feeling in retirement is your mind and body telling you that you need to change your situation. The elements you need to be happy are missing. You can view this as an insurmountable task, or you can work on finding out what needs to be changed. This doesn't mean that you have to go back to work. But it does mean that you've got to ignite your creative side and explore areas in yourself that are unique to you.

You have gifts not found in others that can be developed and then shared. Sometimes it takes a lot of effort to figure this out. Disenchantment and even melancholy can be viewed as gifts that get you moving toward a more enjoyable life. These feelings can be very uncomfortable, but they force us to make changes. If we don't, we can fall into severe depression and possibly despair. We don't want that to happen, so it takes introspection and action to prevent this downward spiral.

Getting to know yourself and caring for yourself gives you the chance to become more authentic in your life. Through introspection, I learned that I had a compulsion to stay busy, and that I was mostly concerned with the outcome and not the process. This compulsion was due to anxiety about not being productive. For me, it was a form of addiction because if I wasn't doing something all the time, I would get nervous and cast around for something to do.

This compulsiveness is hard to break, but I'm working on simply enjoying the process rather than being fixated on any goal. I'm also trying to learn from my experiences, even the bad ones. If we look at melancholy as a signal that we need to make important changes, and then we make those changes that result in a happier life, we'll realize that the melancholy was actually a blessing.

Most people, however, will not view melancholy as such, so they may seek medication, or self-medicate, to relieve their distress. This response will only prolong the melancholy, unless some form of intro-spection is concurrently going on. You may not believe it, but melan-choly can turn out to be your friend. We all have had uncomfortable feelings that have forced us to change.

You may have had to live with and depend on your parents at some point in the past because you didn't have a job. The uncomfortable feeling that you were mooching off your folks probably forced you out of your comfort zone and into the working world. In the end, you were happy when you finally became independent; it boosted your self-es-teem and confidence.

PMS works from the same concept. The disenchanted or melan-choly feeling is nudging you to create a different life. It's telling you to take the time to figure out what's best for you. No one can do this for you because everyone is different; what works for someone else most likely won't work for you.

Some people may not recognize the melancholy of retirement as an indication of the need for change. They may require something more concrete to start the change process. Don't wait for a crisis to occur before you start living the life you want. Disillusionment with retirement may be the wakeup call you need to work on the changes required for a more enjoyable life.

### Failure to Heed Crucial Warning Signs

Throughout our lives, we're constantly overcoming obstacles and challenges, but certain events smack us upside the head and make us take notice. It may take a health problem or the death of someone close to us to spur us to reevaluate our priorities. As mentioned earlier, my wife's surgery shocked me into reality and got me thinking about what was most important in life. I came to terms with the fact that I wasn't living the life I wanted, and that having more time to be with the people I loved, and to do the things important to me, was what I needed.

That was my wakeup call. We all encounter events that goad us into changing something in our lives. If we ignore these signals, they just get more intense. It's wise to try to recognize this issue before something major happens and forces us to change. I saw this with colleagues—they would overwork to the point of mental and physical exhaustion and not recognize they were in trouble. Then they had a major health crisis and were forced either to cut back or retire.

I saw numerous patients over the years who had to make big decisions after suffering a preventable heart attack or stroke. While they were recuperating, they had the time to review their lives and realize how things could have gone differently if they had heeded the warnings. The event had now changed their lives forever and there was no going back. They came to understand that life is very short and time is extremely precious.

Our minds and bodies are constantly giving us signals when we're doing things counter to our nature. In my case, I developed a focal dystonia and was getting intermittent and unexplainable rashes. My sense of humor was plummeting, and I felt tense and anxious a lot of the time. These were signals that I was heading for cataclysmic problems. Luckily, I recognized that a change was needed, so I acted.

The signals could come in many forms. It may be that you're drinking more alcohol than usual, smoking more, sleeping less, gaining weight, or becoming increasingly irritable. It's important to ask ourselves questions about our behavior. Trying to figure it out and then doing something about it should be the goal. I can assure you that money and other external things will not replace your health and well-being once they're lost. In short: don't ignore, explore.

Having problems in retirement is an indication that we may have disregarded earlier signals that our lives were going astray and we were heading down the wrong path. By identifying too much with work, not developing other interests, and not paying enough attention to the physical and mental signs occurring, we set ourselves up for retirement difficulties. Nurturing unhealthy and hard-to-break ways to cope with stress while working can cause people to flounder in retirement. If you are not yet retired, you can start to work on changing some of these behaviors now. If you are already retired, you can't change the past, but you can build a better future. Keep reading to find out how.

### Questions for Reflection

1) How balanced is your life?

2) Do you have hobbies that lead to positive growth?

3) What is/was your relationship with your job? Were you overinvested in it?

4) How do you feel when you are not working?

5) What could you be doing that would lead to positive growth?

6) Do you know anyone who has not adjusted well to retirement? Why the poor adjustment?

℞

## Chapter Three
# Anticipate and Plan for Retirement While You're Still Working

SOME PEOPLE THINK that everything will take care of itself once they retire. They will travel, play golf, and have fun. Life will be great, and they will live happily ever after.

Imagine the shock when things don't turn out the way you thought they would. You may travel for a few months or play golf daily for a few weeks, but then the novelty wears off; you become bored and start to wonder what comes next. That's the problem with having unrealistic expectations, and it's why it's so important to become informed about retirement so you learn what to expect.

I'm confident that the steps recommended in this book will cure or significantly improve PMS. As with any disease, prevention is always better.

### *Plan for Retirement While Still Working*

It's good to start thinking well in advance about what you want your retirement to look like and what you want to do. You can do anything you're capable of doing, but you've got to do something. You get to design the rest of your life, so give it a lot of thought. Many things in your life have likely been neglected because you were too busy working to take care of them. It's up to you to decide how you want to approach your future situation. Working on a plan while you're still employed is a good idea. Thinking about new interests you want to pursue can really help you later on.

I realize that most young, working people would not be interested in doing this type of reflection. They're at a different stage in life. They probably wouldn't see the benefit, but the earlier a person starts, the better. Given that you're reading this, you're either interested in the subject or nearing retirement, so you're probably more open to putting a plan together.

Before I retired, I would ask my retired patients whether they had any regrets or whether they would do anything differently knowing what they then knew. Most said they wished they would have saved more money for later in life and that they had spent more time with loved ones. I also asked whether they would have retired earlier if they'd had the chance. Most of the elderly women and at least half of the men said yes. A small percentage said they would have worked longer for financial reasons.

The majority of women said that if you can afford to retire and have other things you want to do, get busy and do them. A lot of these patients were elderly and had been through major losses. These talks got me thinking about how short life can be and reminded me there's no way to predict the future. If you put off doing what you most want to do, you may never get a chance to do those things. Or a loved one could get ill and prevent your plans from ever materializing. Working in medicine gave me insight into how people's lives can change at the drop of a hat. I saw numerous times how patients had to change their plans because of illness or the death of a loved one. We never know when a life-altering event may occur.

### Evaluate Your Expectations

It's hard to plan for something that may seem like a long way off, but planning should start while you're still working. The first step is to determine what expectations you already have for retirement. The next step is to think about a possible timetable. You can begin to determine your expectations by asking yourself the following questions.

- Are you expecting to retire completely, or do you plan to phase out your work schedule slowly?
- Is another career a possibility?
- What hobbies and interests do you want to pursue?
- What are your talents and strengths?

- Do you have an interest in a particular cause and want to volunteer?
- How are you going to replace the benefits you've derived from your work?
- Are the significant people in your life on the same page concerning retirement?

These are all important questions that take time to answer and shouldn't be ignored.

### *What Is Your Timetable?*

What is your likely timetable? When would you like to retire? At your expected retirement age or before? Do you want to get out at the top of your game or keep going until there's a more concrete reason to leave? When do people in your field commonly retire? Is there a mandatory retirement age? What would you do if you were forced to retire? It's good to have answers to these questions so you are prepared and have a timeframe in mind.

Once you become financially independent, it's really your call. Some people get caught up in telling themselves, "Just one more year and then I'll retire." The year comes and goes, no retirement plans have been made, and the cycle begins again. Setting a plan in motion doesn't mean you can't change the plan if need be, but it helps to reduce your anxiety about the future. Some people can't imagine themselves retired, so just thinking about it causes anxiety. Setting a timetable helps you to deal with that anxiety. Nothing relieves anxiety better than planning and preparation. Or would you rather let circumstances determine when you retire? Once you realize you are financially capable of retiring, your timetable may change.

Remember that what you think and feel today will most likely not be what you're thinking or feeling five years or even a year from now. When I started out as a doctor, I didn't think I would ever retire, but after nearly three decades, my attitude changed significantly. Even after a decade of working, I noticed a change in my ideas about retirement.

I'm certain that your attitude about your job will change over time. At some point, you may no longer enjoy the work you do. You may have to keep coming up with innovative ways of changing your job in order to remain interested.

Establishing a retirement time may seem like a big ordeal, but it's not. Setting aside a few minutes a week to start the planning is all you need. Discussing your timeline with your loved ones will help ensure you're all on the same page.

I decided to leave pretty much at the top of my career. My interest in my work was beginning to wane, and I knew the quality of my work would probably decline if I continued working. I didn't like that feeling, so I decided to leave. Some people continue to do decent work even after their interest has declined, but that was not my situation.

It's important to know when it's time to quit. Some people continue to work even when they're not doing an adequate job. A lot of jobs have no mandatory retirement age so people can continue to work as long as they desire. That's a good thing when people are capable and have maintained their skill levels. The problem arises when people don't realize or are in denial about the loss of competency. Staying on the job does them, their employers, and society no favors by continuing to work under those circumstances.

We need to be honest with ourselves and do the right thing when we can no longer perform high quality work. When your interest in and dedication to your job starts to decline, it's time to think about leaving, or at least reducing or changing your responsibilities. If you can no longer physically or mentally do the job, it's time to depart. If there is some way to improve your attitude or skills and you want to stay on the job, then do so.

### Try Retirement on for Size

Your identification (or over-identification) with work is probably the hardest aspect of retirement to deal with. If your job is your source of identity, self-worth, and self-esteem, you lose that when you retire. The power and influence you once possessed is now someone else's. It's difficult for us not to identify with our jobs because we've spent years working our way through the ranks and becoming proficient in what we do. If your friends and social life are made up of colleagues from work, or if you have no hobbies or interests outside of work, your job has taken over your identity and life. Only by recognizing this situation can you start to make changes.

I remember when I first started developing hobbies unrelated to my work. It felt very foreign to me. I felt guilty and feared I would fall behind in my profession. This barrier was difficult to break through, but it also opened the door for other interests.

Once that door was opened, I found that I enjoyed my new interests as much as working, and they didn't have any negative effect on my job performance. Problems arose when the opposite happened—work started getting in the way of my interests. This situation wasn't supposed to happen, but it showed me how much I was enjoying my new interests. I finally realized how many things there are that we can do to add variety and enjoyment to life. It's also good to start developing friendships outside of work; they will provide you with a diverse and supportive network when you retire.

I know now that one's experience of life should be broad and diversified. It's like investing—if you're overly invested in one area, you're likely to get hurt. You should put your money in a variety of investments and your time in several interests.

While you're still working, try to imagine not having your job and pay attention to how you feel. Doing this exercise may give you an idea of how strongly you're attached to your job and help you to prepare for the transition.

You can also try retirement on for size before you retire. Taking an extended vacation while you're still working can provide insight into how retirement might feel. If you're antsy after just a few days off from work, you may want to address this and understand why. If you're relaxed and don't seem to miss work, you might do better with retirement's unstructured time. But unless you can take several months off, a vacation may not be a true indication of retirement life.

If a long weekend just about drives you nuts, you'll have problems with retirement, unless you deal with those problems beforehand. Pay attention to your feelings when you have time off. Is it easy to occupy your time? Do you really enjoy your time off, or are you just going through the motions? You'll have much more free time during retirement, so it's vital that you address this issue while you're still working.

You also should consider whether you want to work part-time for a while before you completely retire. You might even want to do consulting work in your field.

If you haven't retired yet, it's a good idea to start developing new and multiple identities. For example, father, friend, community member, church participant, artist, musician, volunteer, etc. How we feel about ourselves is the most important factor in a successful retirement. If we feel useless, irrelevant, and worthless, our moods and lifestyle will reflect this. If we feel we're as worthy as anyone else and have value by just being alive, retirement will be a much happier experience.

### *Evaluate Your Beliefs about Retirement*

Life is to be enjoyed and lived to the fullest, but life is not meant to be fun and games all the time. There are going to be ups and downs. Some people, before they retire, view retirement as an escape from the rat race and eternal bliss. This outlook is unrealistic and can often lead to disappointment once retirement occurs.

No matter how prepared you are, you'll still be thrown a few curveballs. The more time you devote to learning about retirement, the more realistic you can be about your expectations. Sometimes things turn out better than expected, but if your expectations are too high, you're bound to be disappointed.

Our beliefs can get in the way of a good retirement. We may believe that we should keep working until we can't do the job anymore. This belief is deeply rooted in our work ethic and is hard to overcome. It's been ingrained in us for many generations. In the past, it was very important that everyone had a job to do. Times have changed, however, and society is less dependent on everyone working for the duration of his or her life. Today you can retire at any time if you can support yourself financially.

The belief that everyone needs to keep working forever is outdated, so let it go. You may, in fact, be helping society by retiring, because it allows you the opportunity to become happier, healthier, and to be an example for the younger generations. You might also be opening up a job for someone else who needs employment. So your beliefs may need to change in this regard if you're going to avoid problems. Having conflicted beliefs about work and retirement will most likely lead to a lot of emotional turmoil for you. This subject will be discussed at length in subsequent chapters.

### *Spend Time Imagining and Reflecting Upon Your Retirement*

Spend some time imagining what your ideal retirement would be like. Imagine what a typical day would be like when you're retired. Work through every detail. What time will you get up? How will you use your time during the day? If you're having trouble coming up with things you'd like to do, it's time to come up with ideas. Make a list of things you would like to do if you had more time and then pursue the ones that most interest you. Using your imagination to go through a typical day of retirement will reveal what you need to work on now.

Start taking the time to reflect on your life. Are you living the life you want? Are you happy in your work and relationships? What would you change if you could?

Because our lives become so busy at times, we may lose sight of what's important to us. If we work on being more reflective, we're more likely to recognize where and how our lives have gone off-track. If we have neglected doing this reflective work for a long time, it will take practice.

Not many things feel worse than the sensation that you've not lived the life you would have liked. It's never too late to make adjustments, but it's certainly better to start early in planning the life you want to live.

### *Become Aware of Your Workaholic Tendencies*

The workaholic and retirement go together like a boat and the desert. The compulsion to work long hours is caused by an underlying problem. It could be anxiety, depression, or a self-esteem issue. The causes are many and varied. Excessive work distracts us from dealing with the underlying issue, allowing it to go unresolved. It is like an infection that is allowed to fester and later requires surgery to drain. Sorry; my medical background seeps through sometimes, but you get the point. It just gets worse.

When a workaholic retires, that long-suppressed issue comes out in full bloom and is difficult to manage. The workaholic will then try to control the problem with some other compulsion or distraction. A new addiction can replace the old.

I can relate to this dilemma. When I was a doctor, I was on call a lot; that meant I had to be available all day and through the night. I discovered that I couldn't relax when I was on call, so I regularly had a sense of anxiety. I believe I have always had low grade anxiety, but having to be available those twenty-four hours made it worse. I learned that if I worked longer and harder while on call, the anxiety was not as noticeable. My mind was occupied with work and not with what I was feeling. Eventually, I was working more and sleeping less.

When I retired from medicine, I no longer had work as a means for masking the anxiety, and that made the adjustment to retirement more challenging. If you have workaholic tendencies, start to become more aware of this problem. Cut back on your work schedule and deal with the problems in a healthier way. Accept the fact that you may need professional help to identify the root cause of the work addiction. If the compulsion to work continues, it can be devastating to your health and relationships. If you find that you're working more than eight hours a day and your family time is markedly reduced, or that you've lost touch with friends and important relationships, you may have a problem. Recognize that you do and start to rectify it.

### Be Aware of Changing Feelings Toward Your Job

Over time, our feelings about our jobs may change. What fascinated us before may now seem routine and mundane. This change is common and will almost certainly happen to you at some time in your career. It may be an indication that you need a change and more time to enjoy the life you have. Don't ignore these feelings—they're trying to tell you something. This is a warning sign that something needs to change; it may be as simple as changing your outlook or as major as retiring from your current situation.

Burnout is also very common, and it may not be your fault. Sometimes blame is directed at the person suffering from burnout—he or she is felt to be weak or to lack stamina. More likely, the person just got overextended and now can't handle the situation. But the burnout may also be due to the job situation and the excessive or even unrealistic expectations put on the employee. Being burnt out on the job sets you up for a whole host of problems. These problems can include mental and physical health issues and possibly an earlier-than-anticipated exit from the workforce. Keep this in mind because an untimely departure from your job could financially affect the quality of your retirement.

If you're having symptoms of burnout, such as fatigue, disinterest in your job, or depression, talk with your employer to see how the situation can be changed as soon as possible. No job is worth your emotional or physical health. A job can be replaced, but your health, once damaged, may be harder or impossible to repair. Don't expect your employer to tell you to slow down and get more rest or to take all your accumulated vacation time. Your health is your responsibility, so it's up to you to protect it.

We never know when a life-changing event may occur, so the joy of working at your current job could end at any time. That's why it's important to be thinking about retirement before it's forced on you or before you say you've had enough. Try to get a handle on any workaholic tendencies and be aware of any signs of burnout. Ignoring these potential problems can make an enjoyable retirement more difficult. Learning about your beliefs and expectations and any potential snares can help ensure you start your retirement on the right foot. It's not possible to anticipate every potential problem, but if you will start brainstorming what could conflict with your ideal retirement, you'll have less pitfalls to deal with when retirement comes. One of those pitfalls can be mistaking your wants for needs during retirement. We'll cover that topic in the next chapter.

## *Questions for Reflection*

1) Do you have workaholic tendencies?

2) What would your friends say about the amount of time you spend with them?

3) Are you able to get out of the work-mode when on vacation?

4) Do you take days off and use all of your vacation time?

5) Are most of your relationships work-related?

6) Do you feel better at work or away from work?

R̶X

## Chapter Four
# Understand the Difference Between
# Wants and Needs

To HELP YOU understand the difference between needs and wants, an understanding that is crucial to a healthy retirement, let's look at a hypothetical example. We have two children who are both less than a year old. We put the first child in a room and give him a beautiful red ball to play with. After ten minutes, we take away the ball and give him a rattle. He begins to cry and fuss because he isn't interested in the rattle and wants the ball back. After a minute of crying, the rattle is replaced with a green ball. The child keeps crying, still wanting the red ball that was taken away. The green ball is taken away and the child is given nothing to play with. He continues to cry, still upset about the missing red ball.

The second child faces the same situation. She's given the red ball, which she plays with and enjoys, and then it's taken away. She's then given the rattle, which she enjoys before it is taken away. She's then given the green ball; once again, she plays with it before it's taken away. Left with no toys, she starts observing her surroundings. She plays with her feet, laughs, and seems to enjoy herself.

Would you rather live your life as the first child or the second one? The first child lost any ability for joy after the red ball was taken away. No amount of crying or fussing was going to bring it back. For some of us, leaving our jobs is like losing the red ball. That is not to imply that we are just big babies, but it's important to understand that no amount of sadness will bring back your work situation. No emotion, whether happy or sad, will change the fact that you are no longer working at your job. So why not choose happiness when you lose something in life? Why not accept the change and work on making the most of it? You'll feel better about your situation and be able to find other things you can enjoy instead.

Remember the story I told earlier about Mr. Smith, my patient in the nursing home who said he was very happy? His example shows that once our basic needs are met, life is just an attitude thing. That would mean that everything else in our lives is superfluous. We can do without the big house, fancy car, exotic vacations, and even the feelings we derive from our jobs.

### Distinguish Between Needs and Wants

Once you're aware of all the things you don't really need, you'll gain insight into the difference between wants and needs. If you can't differentiate between the two, you will need a lot to keep you happy. I want you to get down to the basics here. Think about it: If you were to lose all your possessions and your health, essentially everything except your bare minimum basic needs, would you still be able to muster up some happiness? This situation may never happen and probably won't, but it's good to know that you could maintain happiness even after a significant loss.

We may lose our health, possessions, money, family, entertainment, etc. Could you be happy even if you lost your looks or your hearing? Think about and try to list everything you feel you need to be happy. Start by considering what you already have that you will continue to require to be happy. The greater your list of needs, the more potential there is for unhappiness. If we're prepared to understand that most things we think we need aren't necessary to a happy life, we'll have much less disruption in our lives. You may also find that most of the things you have listed are not needs but actually wants.

Once your basic needs are met, there is really only one need essential for a fulfilling life, and that is for you to be accepting of yourself— to be who you are, your authentic self, to use the gifts and talents you were born with in your own unique way, and to live the life you were meant to live. This allows you to reach your potential while doing the things you have the natural ability to do.

I didn't come up with this concept of wants and needs myself; it was professed by an American psychologist named Abraham Maslow. He created Maslow's Hierarchy of Needs, which shows that once our basic needs are met, we need to become who we really are. It is not optional. We need to become who we are in order to have a fulfilling life. As I see it, the problem is not being who we really are. The difficulty arises with letting go of who we aren't—the person we think we are and are projecting to others. Some people get stuck because they are not aware of this concept and feel the need to acquire more in the realm of the basic needs. They exhibit this behavior through more shelter in the form of multiple homes or one very large abode, greater amounts of food, or more money. These people will never be fulfilled because they will never reach the top level of the hierarchy and never become who they truly are. You are less likely to have a happy and satisfying life if you don't use the attributes unique to you.

It can be difficult trying to figure out who we are after many years or even a lifetime of being somebody other than our true selves. Many will not want to put in the effort required. Remember that our basic needs will need to remain met in order to reach the higher levels of needs, such as self-esteem, health, and financial wellbeing. How to achieve these higher levels will be discussed in future chapters.

It seems to me that it is a waste of life to have lived separately from who we really are, and to have let the unique qualities, found in all of us, remain dormant. Happiness is more a state of mind, and I think it is nearly impossible to be happy if we are not able to be who we truly are. Once we become our true selves, we can stop trying to be happy and just choose to be happy.

Below is Maslow's Hierarchy of Needs, which is generally depicted as a pyramid with Self-Actualization as the pinnacle. At the base are our basic physiological needs, followed by safety, then belonging/love and then esteem. These basic needs must to be met before advancing to the need for self-actualization. This means that if the basic needs are not met, then self-actualization is unlikely to take place. People can also become mired in the lower needs and never reach self-actualization. In other words, they have the resources and ability to become who they really are, but they are lacking the proper mindset. Included also are several quotes from Abraham Maslow that reinforce the concepts and recommendations in this book. I was going to limit the quotes to two or three, but I feel they all carry an important message for the reader and are consistent with what I am trying to convey.

Self-Actualization
Esteem Needs
Belonging and Love Needs
Safety Needs
Physiological Needs

*Maslow's pyramid puts Self-Actualization*
*at the pinnacle of our needs*

"If you deliberately plan to be less than you are capable of being, then I warn you that you will be deeply unhappy for the rest of your life. You will be evading your own capacities, your own possibilities."

"If the essential core of the person is denied or suppressed, he gets sick sometimes in obvious ways, sometimes in subtle ways, sometimes immediately, sometimes later."

"It looks as if there were a single ultimate goal for mankind, a far goal toward which all persons strive. This is called variously by different authors self-actualization, self-realization, integration, psychological health, individuation, autonomy, creativity, productivity, but they all agree that this amounts to realizing the potentialities of the person, that is to say, becoming fully human, everything that person can be."

"A musician must make music, an artist must paint, a poet must write, if he is to be ultimately at peace with himself. What a man can be, he must be."

"One can choose to go back toward safety or forward toward growth. Growth must be chosen again and again; fear must be overcome again and again."

"I can feel guilty about the past, apprehensive about the future, but only in the present can I act. The ability to be in the present moment is a major component of mental wellness."

"Self-actualized people...live more in the real world of nature than in the man-made mass of concepts, abstractions, expectations, beliefs and stereotypes that most people confuse with the world."

"The key question isn't 'What fosters creativity?' But why in God's name isn't everyone creative? Where was the human potential lost? How was it crippled? I think therefore a good question might not be why do people create? But why do people not create or innovate?
"We have got to abandon that sense of amazement in the face of creativity, as if it were a miracle that anybody created anything."

"The great lesson is that the sacred is in the ordinary, that it is to be found in one's daily life, in one's neighbors, friends, and family, in one's backyard."

"Be independent of the good opinion of other people."

"Let people realize clearly that every time they threaten someone or humiliate or unnecessarily hurt or dominate or reject another human being, they become forces for the creation of psychopathology, even if these be small forces. Let them recognize that every person who is kind, helpful, decent, psychologically democratic, affectionate, and warm, is a psychotherapeutic force, even though a small one."

Carl Gustav Jung was a Swiss psychiatrist who said, "The persona is that which in reality one is not, but which oneself as well as others think one is."

It is important to know that when a person uses his or her talents and abilities it doesn't have to be on a grand scale or at a professional level. Just using the individual gifts and talents that he or she has is the key.

Anything beyond the basics certainly has the potential to make our lives more exciting, pleasurable, and fun. Your job would fit into this category. It may have brought you some joy and helped support you and your family, but it is expendable.

The more you want, the greater the difficulty in maintaining your happiness. If you view your looks as a need, it's going to be very costly and time-consuming to try to keep them up (not to mention the difficulty you'll have when your looks fade). I can remember not recognizing patients who didn't have in their false teeth, hadn't dyed their hair, or weren't wearing makeup. They needed a lot of work and effort to maintain their appearances. It's good to look your best, but realize that your looks can go at any time and that you have the ability to accept that.

If you know your wants and needs, and there's not much of a gap between the two, you're better able to concentrate on those parts of your life most important to your happiness. Your needs are what you feel are absolutely required for you to live. They include the basic needs—food, water, shelter, and socialization (which would include companionship, intimacy, and reproduction)—but also your individual needs that you find unexpendable. We all want more than just our very basic needs, but some things and situations are not necessary for us to live a happy life, even though we think they are.

Just remember that whatever you think is mandatory for happiness becomes a condition on your happiness and will need to be maintained for you to remain happy. If your happiness is dependent on being entertained, but entertainment becomes unavailable, your happiness will be disrupted. So, think about only those things you truly need to have peace of mind. Once you determine what they are, you can devote your time and energy to having them during retirement.

Let's now approach our needs with nature in mind. Everyone would agree that we're a part of nature, right? If you don't agree, just look at our anatomy and that of most animals; it's very similar. If you have dissected an animal, or witnessed it being done, you know we have the same organs. Have you ever seen an obese deer in the wild? Have you ever seen an animal with extras like jewelry or anything showy? No, because that would slow it down and put it at higher risk of being another animal's lunch. Fauna in the wild require very little to satisfy their basic needs—food, shelter, and socialization. Wild animals use only what they need to survive, not more or less. These animals spend most of their day trying to meet those survival needs.

We humans have figured out how to have our basic needs met, and rather than having to scurry around for food and shelter, we have the time to pursue other things. We don't have to keep trying to meet the basic needs, by accumulating more, when those basic needs are already met.

In retirement, our basic needs will most likely be met, and this will free up a lot of time for personal growth. This can be an opportunity for great positive growth in the form of discovering our talents and gifts. Unfortunately, it is used by some for participation in activities resulting in negative growth.

Nature teaches us that all living creatures must continue with some form of positive growth (not necessarily in width) and that resources should be utilized efficiently. Comprehending the truth of this situation is tough because nature tells us one thing while human nature gives us a different message. It is a schizophrenic picture. If we follow human nature, we will believe that more is better, but according to Mother Nature, just enough is better. It all boils down to which nature you think is right. As you can see by what is going on in the world, we humans don't always make the best decisions. I put my trust in Mother Nature, which has been around for billions of years. How about you?

We are part of this animal kingdom, so our basic needs are very similar. Remember: Having more than we need goes counter to nature, and the only way to command nature is to obey it. We are only separated from the rest of the animal kingdom by our powerful, unique, and diversified minds. We will talk about that in a future chapter. My point is that we don't need a lot of extras to be happy, and sometimes the extras can be a hindrance.

We can break it down even further. Sometimes discerning between a want and a need can get confusing, and there can be an overlap. Let's say you are hungry and need to eat. Do you need a steak and lobster, or can a less expensive, healthier meal fulfill that need? Basic food is a need, but steak and lobster are wants. The same applies to the other basic needs that we have, including shelter and socialization.

Most people wouldn't want to live with just the bare basics, and you don't have to. At the same time, it's good to get a perspective on what your basic needs would be just in case you lose some of what you have today. The true basics can still bring you happiness if you have the right attitude.

I'm not asking you to make a list of all the things you need to be happy for financial reasons, although differentiating between your wants and needs can be of financial benefit if it leads to you spending less. What I am asking you to do is to recognize things you don't need so you are prepared if in the future you don't have them, and so you can reduce the items in your life that may be cluttering it up and working as obstacles to your happiness in retirement. In the next section, we'll discuss how to recognize things we don't need and how to get rid of them.

### *Reduce Clutter and Obligations in Your Life*

Before we retire, it's good to start reducing the clutter we have built up in our lives. I don't mean just the goods we have accumulated, although it's wise to start eliminating the things we don't need or use. We should also look into the activities that are just wasting our time.

Everything we do requires an exchange. When we give a lot of time and energy to an activity, that time isn't available to do other things that are possibly more beneficial for us. The goal here is to lighten the load. When you retire, you're going to need time to adjust to and explore your options. Try to figure out why you feel you need to continue the relationship or situation that isn't working.

Too many burdening obligations will make it harder to adjust to retirement. Activities may seem, at least on the surface, to be helpful because they occupy your time and get your mind onto something else. But they may only delay the process of adjusting to retirement, and then that time is lost.

So, start reducing your obligations. If you're a member of an organization or committee and you no longer enjoy it, resign and fill the time with something more useful and pleasurable. It's possible you joined certain groups to advance your career, but now that's no longer necessary. Sometimes it's very difficult to say no, but it's the best thing to do if you aren't really interested in the group. The organization probably wasn't benefiting from your lack of interest. There is no need to continue activities that are no longer useful to you. Replace them with activities you feel are more important in meeting your true needs.

Most of us feel we need more rather than less, but I'm here to tell you from experience that you can be comfortable with less than you think. We all know on some level that wanting more and getting more doesn't satisfy us, but we keep doing it anyway. We keep attempting to satisfy our empty feelings with more stuff, more excitement, or more whatever, but that only leads to a never-ending cycle of frustration and disappointment. Instead, try to live with fewer material goods and obligations than you currently have and see how much happier you might become.

For example, if something you own breaks, see if you can live without it rather than replacing it. Do you really need a new watch if yours stops running, especially if you have a cellphone you carry with you everywhere? If you no longer have to drive to work every day, then maybe if your car dies, you could consider just walking or taking a cab when you need it.

This exercise of learning to live with less is not meant to make you feel worse. It will help you to challenge your assumptions and to change deeply ingrained beliefs. It will teach you to appreciate what you already have while you have it, and it will give you more confidence about handling whatever life throws your way.

Start cutting back on purchasing more material things. They can drain a lot of your energy. Trying to maintain items you don't need or use can cost you valuable time and money. Lighten the load and get rid of what you aren't using.

It can get to the point where you don't own your stuff; rather, it owns you. It ties you down and restricts your freedom. Sometimes our garages, attics, and basements are full of stuff we hardly use; we may not even know what's in that garage. Take inventory and unload that unused stuff before and after you retire; it will allow you to be more nimble and flexible.

We can never imagine all the possible scenarios we may encounter, but we can come to terms with losing everything we have and still remaining happy. If you're able to do that, your appreciation of life will be forever changed. You'll view life from a perspective of abundance rather than lack.

This, of course, is done in your mind. You don't have to give up anything or deprive yourself of anything after you do this exercise, but you may notice that you're more comfortable in wanting less. It's truly the simple things in life that make us happy. Life is not supposed to be one exciting thing after another. Life is just life, and the sooner we understand that, the better.

It may take time for you to understand the power of this mental exercise, but the outcome will be worth the effort. If you don't see the benefit right away, don't worry; living with less is so opposed to what we've been led to believe that it takes time to accept it. So, see whether it makes sense and is beneficial to you; if not, let it go and try again when you're more receptive to the idea.

As I've stated before, you don't have to change your life. Rather, it's important to change the way you look at life and your approach to dealing with it. Imagine living with less and observe how your outlook changes. Don't worry—you won't lose your motivation for living; in fact, embracing a simpler life should be freeing, reduce stress, and lead to greater peace.

If you're having trouble understanding this concept or you feel angry with just the suggestion of living more simply, you may want to ask yourself why. Why is this subject so hard to address? Why does it touch a nerve with you? Preparing for retirement means gaining insight into our attitudes and assumptions. What we gain in wisdom and understanding now will be invaluable when we are no longer working.

Too often we distract ourselves so we don't have to face unpleasant subjects. Most of us don't want to deal with loss. But if we face our losses, we can disarm them. We'll then be less apt to fear loss and handle it better when it occurs. We cannot prepare for or anticipate every loss we'll face, but if we understand that loss is inevitable and that everyone must face it, we won't be paralyzed by fear of it.

You certainly can't enjoy your life if you're mourning your losses. You can't enjoy the process of living and your individual journey if you're lamenting the past.

To a lesser degree, we also potentially do harm to ourselves by trying to reach certain unrealistic goals. We put ourselves under a lot of unnecessary stress and then have health issues develop. So living a less demanding life is a viable option. A lot of the stress we have is self-imposed. Some of our financial stresses develop because we have overextended ourselves. The majority of our health issues are life-style-related. We don't have to live like monks to have a more relaxed and contemplative life. Most people would agree that a monk's life is not that appealing. However, you can live a partial monk's life (PML), which means not living with a lot of extraneous situations, activities, or possessions.

We can work to declutter our external lives by getting rid of the things we don't need and not buying unnecessary items. We can eliminate unhealthy behaviors and incorporate healthy ones. Next, we can work on decluttering our internal lives by getting rid of negativity and unhealthy thoughts and actions. Eliminate dishonesty, gossip, and greed. We'll discuss how to do this in more detail in upcoming chapters.

The key point is that you can reduce some of the clutter, both internal and external, and still have a great life. In my opinion, a much better life.

### Be Prepared to Accept Life's Inevitable Losses

I know that I have been talking a lot about losses in life and being able to accept the losses that could happen. But what do you do when the loss does happen? Life is a series of acquisitions and losses, and aging successfully means dealing well with both. We'll eventually lose all that we have acquired, including our lives. Facing this reality and aging gracefully requires emotional flexibility and resilience.

Without those two traits, adaptation is very difficult if not impossible. The good news is that these traits can be learned and enhanced. If our lives are full of stressful and emotional issues at the time of a major change, such as retirement, it may be difficult to develop the flexibility and resiliency needed to adjust. That is why it's important to work on developing these traits beforehand.

With time, your flexibility and resiliency will be tested. Try to approach life with nature in mind. For example, when a flowing stream comes across an obstacle, the water finds a way to go around or under it. It maneuvers whichever way it can, to continue its way to a bigger body of water. The same goes for trees during a windstorm; they bend with the wind to prevent their snapping.

Another example is how plants and animals respond to weather changes and injuries. They either adapt, heal, or perish. Most of us are not flexible and resilient when it comes to changes in our lives, either good or bad. I saw it in my medical practice when people were forced to accept a major loss. Many times, they were not very successful. If we're cognizant of the fact that we need to be more flexible and re-silient, we can start to work to ameliorate this deficiency. This can be achieved by paying attention to how we handle the small, everyday changes that occur in our lives.

Are you handling things in a rigid uncompromising way, or are you able to make adjustments and move on? This will give you an idea of what you need to work on. Another good thing to do is to become aware of some of the changes and challenges other people around you have to deal with. Ask yourself how you would approach the problems that they are having and how flexible and resilient you would be. If your flexibility and resilience are lacking, keep working on it. Just being aware that these attributes are needed is the most important first step. These traits will need to be applied to most of the changes that occur in your life; otherwise, it will be just like what happens in nature, and then our enjoyment of retirement and life will be greatly reduced.

You have the ability to accept loss and change, and you can develop the flexibility and resilience to adapt. So start believing this truth; it will free and empower you to enjoy your life now.

It's not very likely that you'll lose everything, at least not all at once. But by having the belief and knowledge that you can still be happy with only your mind and spirit, you take the bite out of life. Looking at everything, including life itself, as a temporary gift makes you appreciate things more and not take them for granted.

If you master this, you'll have imbued the precious secret known and appreciated by only the dying and those who have suffered major life-changing events. They know what's important in life and what's not that significant. Everything we have has been gifted to us and has a return policy. Appreciate it while you have it, but be prepared to let it go. Here are the five regrets of the dying that Bronnie Ware found through her interactions with patients:

1. I wish I'd had the courage to live a life true to myself, not the life others expected of me.
2. I wish I hadn't worked so hard.
3. I wish I'd had the courage to express my feelings.
4. I wish I had stayed in touch with my friends.
5. I wish that I had let myself be happier.
6. I wish I had more stuff, no cancel that and keep it at five.

## Eliminate Unhealthy Relationships

Hanging around with people we don't like or who are negative can also wear us down and deplete our energy, just like material things and activities can. Negative people are those who are always complaining or whining and have the victim mentality. You may have had to work around a lot of negative people in your career, but now you can choose whom to spend your time with.

Outside of work, you might have negative people in your personal life. It's hard to admit that a relationship or friendship is no longer working, but hanging onto one can be detrimental to our growth. Start paying attention to your emotional reactions when you interact with others. If you feel drained after an encounter with someone, your mind is trying to tell you something.

Non-family relationships that are not working can be stopped. It can be more difficult to get out of a relationship with a family member. If the relationship with this family member is harmful or detrimental to your happiness, you can choose to have no contact or reduce the time you spend with him or her. It is up to you to decide this amount of time, but be aware that you are not obligated to spend time with them.

Work on curtailing the need to spend time with people you don't enjoy or who are chronically negative. Some people may be having hard times or are depressed and appear negative, but they are not negative by nature. These people should be given understanding, compassion, friendship, and time. We will discuss more about toxic people in Chapter Seven.

### Learn to Enjoy the Smaller, Slower Things

Learning to derive pleasure from the little things in life is also extremely important to a fulfilling retirement. We get used to the awards, bonuses, and recognition we receive from work. We also have functions associated with our jobs: dinners, parties, and ceremonies. These events will most likely be absent once you retire. The little pleasures, like spending time quietly at home with family, have been overlooked and taken for granted.

Now is the time to develop your appreciation for the smaller joys in life. Spending time with a significant other or working on a project at home can be very enjoyable, if you learn to be aware and mentally present while doing the activity. Most of our lives are a series of small events with a few bigger events mixed in. Much of the time we're not mentally present when these small, seemingly insignificant moments are occurring; they slip by without us even noticing.

Sometimes when we're with our families, our minds are at work or someplace else. We not only shortchange the people we are with, but we shortchange ourselves as well. The times you once considered insignificant in the past may become those you most remember and treasure. However, creating good memories is only possible if you are fully present in the moment and not mentally somewhere else. You may want to have major and exciting events all the time, but that goal is unrealistic and unnecessary.

Start slowing things down in your life. Don't rush to get things done; try to enjoy the process more. This is an invaluable skill to develop and will really be beneficial in retirement. We have trained ourselves to do things quickly—the faster the better. But speed doesn't always allow us to enjoy the process or even feel pleased when we accomplish or finish our tasks. We rapidly move on to another project or projects and the cycle starts all over again. Slowing down can be learned, but it takes time and awareness. Do you really need to get more done in a shorter period of time?

Along the same lines, give up multitasking and start monotasking. Studies now show that when you multitask, you are more apt to make mistakes and feel more stress. Give your full concentration to one project at a time. Not only will doing so help you obtain control of your life, but your enjoyment will certainly improve and so may your performance. Focusing on one thing won't be easy, but it's worthwhile to become more aware of your work and life patterns and to change what's stressful and unfulfilling.

### Don't Be Bound by Other People's Expectations

Up until now, you may have been living according to other people's expectations. Your parents might have expected you to pursue a certain career path. Your boss may have been expecting you to accomplish certain job performance goals. Your family may be demanding time and support. You may be devoting time to helping people with troubles.

This is all well and good, but as a result, you may have lost track of what's important to you. It's a good idea to start doing the things you want and need to do and to let go of some of the things other people expect you to do. If you're doing an activity to please someone else, you'll derive little satisfaction from it. Activities done out of obligation are not enjoyable and can lead to burnout.

You cannot be all things to all people. If an activity involving other people has become a burden and isn't enjoyable, see whether you can eliminate it. Now is the time to look out for your own happiness. Fill your own cup first and then help others fill theirs. Other people need to be responsible for their own happiness.

Another thing to work on is your assertiveness. When you're retired, you'll have more time available, but friends and family may also try to put demands on that time. The ability to say no is invaluable. It's an art to say no without hurting someone's feelings or feeling guilty, but it can be done. The only way to get your own needs met is to be assertive and set boundaries. Make your own needs a priority.

At work and at home, we may have had the tendency to please others at the expense of ourselves. People-pleasing is a very difficult behavior to change, but it's well worth the effort. Putting other people's needs and wants consistently before your own will lead to both mental and physical problems. That is not to say that you should ignore people or be neglectful, but you do not need to sacrifice your own needs to meet someone else's.

"I cannot give you the formula for success but I can give you the formula for failure—which is: Try to please everybody."
— *Herbert Bayard Swope*

Retirement is your time to live the life you want. You previously may have believed that it is selfish to want to be happy, so you have placed other people's interests before your own. If you have these views and tendencies, become aware of them and work on resolving them. We have to reduce our need for approval and for being needed. It does feel good to help people in need, but when it becomes your sole purpose in life, it may be the result of low self-esteem, which I'll discuss later.

Many people in the caring professions suffer from this problem, resulting in a very unsatisfying life. We make our best contribution to people and society when we're happy with our lives. The ideal situation is to help people because we want to, not because we feel obligated to do so.

Look deeply into the possibility that you might be a people pleaser so you can start to change. You can't help everyone and you certainly won't be liked by everyone, so get used to it. Many people go years or decades without realizing that this is the root of their unhappiness. People pleasing can lead to overwork, fatigue, depression, and a whole array of physical problems. Becoming more assertive will help ensure that you're able to break away from the people-pleasing, codependency lifestyle. You can also use the being RETIRED philosophy I'll discuss in an upcoming section so you can determine what your wants and needs are and then learn to share without having to meet other people's expectations.

So how do you know when you have enough and when you are successful? Let's address these important issues.

### Explore What "Success" and "Enough" Mean to You

We have been discussing wants and needs and being able to recognize the difference between the two. Where do we go from here? An important thing to think about is whether or not you have enough already. It seems that we're always looking to get more. We want more money, more awards, more status. More, more, more. It can be enlightening to come to the realization that you already have enough and don't need to attain more. There's no point in working hard for things at this point in your life that you don't need or even want.

The concept of "enough" can be applied to all aspects of your life. If you have the right amount of money to retire and meet your needs, you have enough. If you've won your share of awards, you have enough. Your "enough level" is going to be different from everybody else's. It's an individual thing and only you can decide the right level for yourself.

This is where your values come in. If you know you have enough money for your needs, you can be happy with what you have and not be troubled. Peer pressure or self-induced pressure "to keep up with the Joneses" is an unwinnable situation. Once you surpass the Joneses, there are still the Rockefellers to tangle with. You can never top everyone, but you can wear yourself out trying. Use this principle in all areas of your life and stick to it. Please try to work on the truth that you are already enough the way you are.

Another value you should explore is your definition of success. What would make you consider yourself a success in life?

Success is certainly different for everyone, and our definition of success will also change as we age. For me, success is having peace of mind and being able to live authentically. Of course, I need a certain amount of material success and self-knowledge to obtain my defined success. Until retirement, I never thought about what success meant to me; I was too busy following society's definition of success. We each should have our own take on what would make us feel successful.

I can't argue with someone who has different goals and different ideas about success because everyone is different. But if you look around, a lot of people with apparent material success are very far from peace of mind and authenticity. It's certainly something to think about.

There is no right or wrong answer, but if you have a better idea of your definition of success, it will be easier to be aware of when you've obtained it. It's fruitless to work hard to attain something just to find out it wasn't what you wanted.

Here are a few thoughts by famous authors and thinkers about how they would define success:

"All you need in this life is ignorance and confidence, and then success is sure."
— *Mark Twain*

"To laugh often and much; To win the respect of intelligent people and the affection of children; To earn the appreciation of honest critics and endure the betrayal of false friends; To appreciate beauty, to find the best in others; To leave the world a bit better, whether by a healthy child, a garden patch, or a redeemed social condition; To know even one life has breathed easier because you have lived. This is to have succeeded."
— *Ralph Waldo Emerson*

"There is only one success—to be able to spend your life in your own way."
— *Christopher Morley*

None of these sayings makes any mention of money, possessions, or fame. I know that working to acquire more and more money and possessions is not going to make you happy or fully successful in life. Some of the people most at peace are not wealthy at all. Remember, all the money in the world will not buy you one second of time. Money and possessions cannot buy your health back once it's lost. Not being satisfied with what we have is somewhat of a delusion, but we all need to discover this on our own.

### Living the Being RETIRED Philosophy

You are, more than likely, going to have unique needs in order for you to enjoy your retirement. This is above and beyond your normal basic needs. You just have to be aware that you can be happy with having your basics needs met if that becomes necessary. As long as you have the capability, you can start to make your personal wants and needs a reality. First, you need to determine what your wants and needs are, and then, you can work on obtaining them. You also should determine where your strengths, talents, and gifts are and how you want to use them. This is where assertiveness becomes beneficial; to meet your needs, you have to have the ability to say no to activities and people who would impede your progress.

After determining what you want out of life and then devising a way to attain it, you need to honor certain personal tenets to make them a reality. The mnemonic to remember here is RETIRED.

R = Responsibility

E = Effort

T = Time Commitment

I = Integrity

R = Reflection

E = Enjoy

D = Distribute/Share

You need to take **Responsibility**, for the task, and realize that only you can bring your unique needs to fruition. Only you can bring to existence the life you desire. It is up to you to take the initiative to begin the change or to start the process.

You also need to be willing to put in the **Effort** to get what you want in your life. Everything worth having takes effort. Just thinking how nice it would be to have something or some change in your life, won't help you. You must take the necessary action.

Another important factor for achieving what you want is to allot the **Time** needed to accomplish your objectives. You will have to protect your time in order to have it available to work on the things you want. Here is where boundaries are so important. Set aside a certain amount of time each day to work on the important things in your life. Make this time a priority for your improvement and be totally committed to maintaining it.

Next is to have **Integrity** in all your actions. No one is going to make sure you are true to yourself. Be honest with yourself and your ability to obtain certain wishes and desires. If certain goals are unattainable, realize it and make adjustments. Don't lie to yourself because that sets you up for failure.

It is always a good practice to **Reflect** on how things are going. When you are pursuing your wants or individual needs, it's beneficial to think about how things are progressing and whether any adjustments need to be made. You may find that you don't like the direction things are going; then take the time to reflect and tweak as necessary.

Don't forget to **Enjoy** the process. If you are not enjoying what you are doing and the changes you are making, you are missing out on what makes life fun and interesting. Ask yourself whether you are deriving enjoyment from the activities you are doing. If you are not, make the necessary corrections. Try not to get discouraged if you are not progressing as fast as you would like. Make the most of the small incremental gains. Even small pebbles can produce vast ripples.

The last thing to do, once you have accomplished the goal, is to **Distribute** it to others. In other words, share what you have learned or some aspect of yourself that will benefit others or society as a whole.

Let's say that, after some contemplation, you determine that in order to be happy, you need to be out with people and interacting. You also note that one of your strengths is that you bond easily with people and you have the ability to communicate with them and make them feel comfortable. You also want to learn a foreign language. You start by taking the responsibility to learn this new language. Then you put in the effort needed to get the books or computer programs, or to sign up for classes. The time needs to be set aside to learn the material and advance toward your goal. You determine that you can put in two hours a day and set the boundaries to do so. It is very important to be honest with yourself about whether you are learning things properly and that this is what you really want.

After a period of time, if you have different feelings about your choices, you have to have the integrity to admit this to yourself. Reflect on how things are going by asking yourself:

- Am I happy with the progress?
- Is this really where my interest is?
- Can I still accomplish the goal in the same time frame?

No experience is going to go well if you are not enjoying the process. If learning a foreign language is not fun and enjoyable, you will not make your best effort. If you are not enjoying the process, make the necessary changes to put yourself back on track. Remember, this is your retirement and the time of your life to learn and put into action those things from which you will derive the most pleasure. Once the foreign language is learned, find ways to share or distribute it to others. Possibly by teaching others or acting as an interpreter. There are many ways to distribute your new knowledge.

This being RETIRED philosophy can be applied to almost anything—even golf. I know a retired executive in my area who loves to fish. He honed his skills and now travels around teaching fishing to local youth. I even applied this philosophy to writing this book. I felt the need to pass on the information I have learned, and I enjoy helping others. Because of the being RETIRED philosophy, the book became a reality.

Taking these actions will result in your positive growth. If you have already developed a talent or one of your gifts, you can still apply it. If you feel you have no gifts or talents to develop, I don't believe you. You can share wisdom, interesting stories, or friendly smiles. You can also use the time to learn and discover who you are and then share your authentic self with the world. This time can be used to figure out why we have adopted certain unhealthy behaviors and what we can do to overcome them. Once we figure out and overcome the problem areas, we can share our knowledge with others who have similar issues. The sky is the limit for where you can use your natural gifts and talents. When you feel fulfilled and purposeful because you are using your natural gifts and talents, you will cure your PMS and experience retirement as the greatest gift of all.

That child, at the beginning of this chapter, didn't need the red ball to be happy. He just hadn't realized that he already had everything he needed to be happy. Hopefully, he is just immature and will realize it long before he retires. So, how many red balls do you need? I hope, after reading this chapter, that you will be starting to think about having less. Just be aware that the need to obtain, possess, and juggle numerous red balls can lead to PMS and possibly temper tantrums.

Remember that by getting your needs and wants sorted out and applying the being RETIRED philosophy, you create positive growth. This positive growth reduces PMS, which allows more positive growth, and the circle continues. With this practice, you are preparing your mind for better thoughts, so your attitude can get set to blast off.

"The richest man is not he who has the most, but he who needs the
least."
— *Author Unknown*

### Questions for Reflection

1) Do you understand the difference between wants and needs?

2) Are you using your natural gifts?

3) Is there a lot of unused stuff in and around your house?

4) Do you belong to any organizations that you don't enjoy?

5) How many needs on Maslow's Hierarchy of Needs have you met?

6) If you just lost your job, how flexible and resilient would you be?
   How could you improve this?

## Chapter Five
# Build Your Identity and Self-Esteem
## on Solid Ground

WHEN WE LEAVE our jobs and retire, we're potentially losing our source of income, status, socialization, and social utility. These losses can be a big blow to our self-esteem and sense of identity. If we retire involuntarily, we may harbor negative feelings about our employer and coworkers, which can add to these feelings. We may feel irrelevant and useless if we were let go from our jobs. Giving up or losing a job can be very stressful. Your life changes the moment you leave your workplace for the last time, and it will never be the same.

Even famous, wealthy people can be jolted when they leave their jobs. David Letterman said at a gala shortly after retiring, "I tell you, if you want to have something affect your self-esteem, retire." Most baby boomers will remember Lee Iacocca, the auto industry mogul of the 1960s to 1980s. In a 1996 interview with *Fortune Magazine*, titled "How I Flunked Retirement," Iacocca said:

> You can plan everything in life, and then the roof caves in on you because you haven't done enough thinking about who you are and what you should do with the rest of your life. Those guys who retire at 53 with early buyouts have a hell of a problem. Actuarially, I've got ten years left. I hope to beat it and do 20. I'm here by myself now, but still optimistic. People ask me why I'm still working so hard. I tell them that without that, and without my kids and grandkids, I'd lose it—I'd have nothing.

These are just two examples, of many, where people who have the financial resources to retire comfortably are not prepared emotionally or psychologically for the big change. Why does this happen? I believe it is most likely due to our feeling good about ourselves when we are working and not so good after leaving work. Ultimately, it is not about the work itself but our personal self-esteem.

It can be difficult to determine the difference between self-esteem, self-worth, and self-concept. Different sources will give you different meanings for these terms, so for simplicity's sake, I will use the word self-esteem specifically according to the definition provided by Nathaniel Branden in his book, *The Six Pillars of Self-Esteem*: "Self-esteem is the disposition to experience oneself as competent to cope with the basic challenges of life and of being worthy of happiness."

I would like to add that it is impossible to have good self-esteem if we don't love and accept ourselves, live our values, challenge our beliefs, and derive our worth from the inside. Unfortunately, most of us derive our self-esteem from the outside. Retirement can cause us to feel badly about ourselves and question what is positive about life.

I feel the main reason many people don't enjoy their retirements is because their self-esteem has taken a big blow. Some of us have never developed self-esteem away from our jobs. We go through school following the crowd and base our self-worth on how we stack up in comparison. We make a career choice based on what our parents say, our peers are doing, or our future income. The self-concept we develop is not on solid ground. We can go through life assuming our self-esteem is doing fine, but then the roof caves in because it has been propped up by artificial means. Our self-esteem is directly related to the thoughts we have about ourselves and our lives, so improving our self-esteem is completely an inside job—it occurs by changing the views we have about ourselves and our lives.

In the rest of this chapter, I'll look at how our self-esteem and identities are affected by retirement, and how we can take steps to improve how we feel about ourselves by forging a new and more authentic identity. We will be discussing how and why our self-esteem is so depleted after retiring and what we can do about it.

## *Feeling Powerless After Retirement*

If you've been the main income-producer in the family and have devoted most of your time to that role, retirement can make you feel powerless. Your breadwinner role is gone, and so is your identity, your self-esteem, and your sense of worth to the family—or so it seems. I say "so it seems" because, in most cases, this perspective is all in your mind.

Your spouse may continue to have a defined role in the home, which makes you feel like you don't belong and aren't needed. Retired Husband Syndrome is a real and global problem. As a result of her husband's retirement, the wife can become depressed and anxious, and she may even begin manifesting physical symptoms. This situation happens because the husband has no family role and starts to encroach on his wife's space, which, in turn, causes the relationship to be stressed. (The same situation could very likely happen in reverse, i.e., Retired Wife Syndrome.) If this problem progresses, it can result in severe unhappiness or even divorce.

What is the answer to this situation? It is important for married couples to be aware that the loss of one spouse's former role can affect that person's self-esteem. To avoid this situation, the establishment of new roles is needed. There will need to be compromises on both spouses' parts and boundaries will need to be set. Here is where communication between family members is needed. Most of the time, it's just a matter of making people aware of your feelings and working on mutually agreed upon solutions. If your feelings of loss are allowed to remain and are not communicated, marital discord can result, further complicating an already dismaying situation. An unresolved problem can lead to worse troubles down the road. That's why it's so important to get in touch with how you're feeling, share those feelings, and then work on solving any problems.

By developing other roles for yourself in the family, you can mitigate those feelings of not belonging. You can become an example for the family of how to deal with change and self-improvement. It takes time for new roles to set in, so don't rush it; just be aware that the change in family dynamics can affect your self-esteem.

You may have neglected your family members when you were working. If so, now is the time to improve those relationships and open the lines of communication. Unresolved family issues can wreak havoc on your self-esteem, and it will be very difficult to have an enjoyable retirement if friction exists between you and your spouse or other family members. The longer these issues go unaddressed, the harder it will be to resolve any differences that have developed over the years. Spend more time with loved ones and get to know them again.

## Feeling Out of Place

Retirees may also feel shunned by society and former colleagues. It's true that some friends, colleagues, and relatives may feel you're not contributing to society anymore, based on their personal beliefs and life situations. You may also have those beliefs, so your self-esteem is riding on them. If you feel your only way to provide value to family and society is when you're employed, it's important to remember *you* create and retain those beliefs. You are most likely exaggerating those negative feelings and forgetting that you have power over how you view your situation.

Some family and friends may even treat you like a second-class citizen because they're fearful of what you're doing or they don't understand your actions because those actions don't adhere to their own belief systems. They also may lack the initiative and creativity to manifest a life other than the one they're living now. However, you can't justify yourself to everyone—that would be part of people-pleasing. Instead, don't let yourself get bogged down by what other people think (or what you think they think). Everyone is on his or her own journey in life. What brings satisfaction for one person may be outside another person's realm of reality. You may need to change your friends and associates and find more like-minded people. In the end, no person's judgment of you can truly affect you unless you allow it. Your self-esteem is not based on what you think people think about you. It's based on what you think about yourself.

Since I've retired, I've discovered that a lot of people are following their own paths. They're living the lives they desire and not caring what others may think and say about their lifestyles. As long as you're happy and not doing anything illegal or hurting anyone else, why should you care if someone else doesn't agree with your choices? We each have our own lives to live, and we are responsible to ourselves and our family. If you can afford to live without being gainfully employed, that's totally up to you.

Sometimes our self-esteem is tied to how we perceive other people as perceiving us. If we think people are accepting us and they appreciate what we are doing, then our self-esteem is high. In turn, when we retire, if we think people don't accept or appreciate us, our self-esteem can plummet. Therefore, we have to separate our self-esteem from what other people might think, say, or do. Don't give your power away.

A patient of mine was sixty-three when she was diagnosed with cancer. Three months prior to being diagnosed, she told me she disliked her job but was going to work until at least age seventy because she didn't have anything else to do. She didn't want to let her fellow workers down, and she also felt she was the only one who could do her job. She was deriving a lot of her self-esteem from others and her job. But when she got her diagnosis, she was forced to retire and make a change she didn't expect. She'd had no previous health problems and had taken extremely good care of herself. The point is none of us has control over what may happen tomorrow or the next day. Life can be very short, so live it to the fullest and don't wait for other people's approval to do so. If we don't create the life we want right now, it may never happen at all.

### Changes from Employed to Unemployed

In many respects, retirement is the exact opposite of being employed. Work provides structure, routine, socialization, utility, status, and income. Retirement provides none of these, although in most cases, it gives you the freedom to find these things on your own and in new ways. It's totally up to you to develop a new structure and routine in retirement. Or you can opt for no structure; it's your call.

The status you have in retirement is dependent on how *you* define it. If you continue to define your status according to how your former workplace would define it, you'll be deeply disappointed. If you have let your self-esteem become dependent on some believed status, you will need to change that in retirement. The status you obtained from work will no longer be present. You may have to examine your own definition of status and to what extent status has been necessary for your happiness. Status is relative, temporary, and can change at any time. We can be at the top of the totem pole one minute and below the ground the next. On your death bed, status is not going to matter much, so why should it be a problem when you retire?

A lot of retirement books recommend replacing lost work with other activities. It doesn't seem to matter what the activity is; the mantra is "Just keep busy." This isn't necessarily a bad plan, but it may prolong your transition through the retirement stages. It's not a good idea to jump into something you really don't like just to occupy your time. If your choice doesn't work out, you are back to square one and with depleted self-esteem. This is your chance to develop yourself in new areas you never had the time to explore before. If you have derived some of your self-esteem from being busy and needed, then you will need to reexamine those needs.

The habits and mindset that allowed you to survive in the workforce for decades may actually be a detriment to your enjoyment of retirement. Your work environment may have been competitive, harried, adrenaline-inducing, and tense. You may have been used to giving orders and having people look up to you to solve major problems. At the end of the day, you felt like you had accomplished something and were needed. If your self-esteem is based on your ability to lead and boss people, that situation will most likely need to change when you retire. You won't be the boss and you probably won't have the sycophants around. Look on this situation as freeing. All eyes are no longer on you to make major decisions. If you think this change might be a problem for you, know that just being aware of it and weaning down on the need always to be the leader can help.

Retirement will only provide you with structure, status, and a new identity if you create them. No one is going to give you a routine to follow, and if you start cranking out commands, I can guarantee you won't get a favorable reaction from family members. A change in your behavior is absolutely necessary and totally your responsibility; it requires a major adjustment in conceptions and expectations. In a sense, retirement means bucking the system because our society places so much emphasis on external things to boost our self-esteem. However, your self-esteem is self-generated and can't be derived from outside sources.

Some of our behaviors can affect and reflect for us how healthy our self-esteem is. Pay attention to your coping and soothing strategies, and be aware if some unhealthy behaviors are escalating. If so, a self-esteem issue may need to be investigated. In my opinion, it all boils down to how we feel about ourselves. If we feel positive about ourselves, we won't become so easily dependent on externals to maintain our self-esteem. If we have negative feelings about ourselves that can cause low self-esteem or be the result of poor self-esteem, this can make the adjustment to retirement that much harder.

Your job was mostly a way of supporting yourself; it is not supposed to be who you are. It is a way for you to share some of your talents, but it does not define you as a person. If you liked your job, that's a plus, but no job lasts forever. The only way you can prevent low self-esteem in retirement is not to associate your self-esteem with your job, in any fashion. Instead, you must derive your self-esteem from the inside. And the only way you can do that is to love and accept yourself totally, live your values, and feel competent at handling life's basic challenges.

### Don't Rely on External Factors for Your Self-Esteem

I mentioned this topic earlier, but it bears repeating. External factors are anything outside yourself—money, possessions, people, relationships, behaviors, you name it. These are all things we can become dependent upon for self-worth. By doing so, we relinquish our power to something outside of us that is impermanent and that could be lost at any time. Everything is temporary, even life itself. Basing our self-esteem on external objects or particular situations is dangerous. If we allow ourselves to be defined by externals, we may never find true happiness. Many of us have lived like this our whole lives and have not realized it.

If you're missing work during retirement, remember that you're not actually missing work but the feelings associated with it. Identifying why you have this feeling is important because an underlying issue may need to be addressed and resolved. Your self-esteem has become dependent on those feelings, so it is hard to give them up. This self-image, which is being propped up, is what you want to project to others and society. It is not necessarily based on who you truly are as a person and your uniqueness. Your job doesn't want you, the person; it wants your talent or ability. It doesn't know or care to know the real you. We may even get to the point where we feel we are that person doing the job. Our true selves get suffocated and are replaced by the idealized person we are on the job. This situation may get to the point where we don't even know who we truly are.

Retirement is the time when we can truly be who we are. Your retirement can be devoted to self-discovery and personal development. The more you've let yourself be defined by something outside yourself, the more challenging this will be. Being anything other than our true selves is difficult to maintain for a lifetime; the effort is taxing and requires a lot of energy, which can lead to stress and anxiety. This situation may explain why a lot of people are so miserable in their jobs. In retirement, we can search for the answer as to why we have had to perpetuate this image and discover just how far we've deviated from our true selves. Don't fret about any deviation you do discover because most of us have followed the same path.

Once you believe that happiness is possible with just the basics of life, you can become more creative with your life. We all have creative abilities, and now is the time to use them. Once you develop the right attitude, your creative abilities should come alive. These creative pursuits will separate you from everyone else because no two people are the same, and they will allow your true self to shine through. Pursuing your creative side and developing new abilities will help you feel competent to meet the challenges facing you in retirement. These actions will certainly bolster your self-esteem because they are generated by you for the sole purpose of enhancing your life and the lives around you.

Once again, expecting external objects or experiences to make you feel good about yourself is a fool's game. They will only make you happy for a short time at best, and you may never be satisfied, always having to search for more. As you get older, you may not be able to afford or maintain the extras. If you've become dependent on them to boost yourself up, but you don't have them or can't acquire them, you most likely won't be happy. You may say, "If I can't have X, then I can never be happy." That may be your belief, but it makes your happiness contingent on the presence of X. Yes, you may be lucky enough to have X and never lose it, but what happens if you do? A better approach is to enjoy whatever it is while you have it, while realizing it's not necessary as the foundation of your present or future self-esteem. This includes your job.

We face a lot of societal pressure to find our value outside ourselves; that's how the economy is structured. The advertising industry wants us to feel like we are inadequate and always lacking something. Then if we buy that car, we'll be happy. If we get a bigger house, our life will be better. Advertising is a ruse to make you feel inferior if you don't have these things. Our society emphasizes self-esteem enhancement through external means. Get good grades so you can get a good job. Work hard to make a lot of money. Own a big house and a big car. These goals are okay as long as they're not the foundation for your self-esteem. While these things can enhance your life, and make it a bit more fun, they can also turn around and bite you in the rear if your self-esteem is totally wrapped up in having them.

If you already have a healthy state of self-esteem, these things aren't needed. You can buy or obtain them only if you need them and will use them. You can make that decision from a position of power. But if you don't really like yourself, you're going to have a hard time resisting the urge to raise your self-esteem with external props.

I'm not implying that you need to live like a pauper, but it's important that you work on and maintain your self-esteem from the inside and not the outside. You're setting the stage for the future by what you're doing today. It's not necessary to become a fanatic about it; just be aware of this issue and start working on improving your relationship with yourself. This process starts with loving and accepting yourself unconditionally.

### Love and Accept Yourself Unconditionally

This concept may sound touchy feely, but you really need to start loving, respecting, and accepting yourself. How we treat ourselves is a direct reflection of how much we care about ourselves. People who tear themselves down physically and mentally don't care much about themselves. If we don't learn to love ourselves, we won't be able to love others. It takes time to learn to love ourselves because we have been taught to put the needs of others above ours. This doesn't make sense; if we don't love or even like who we are, how are we going to do what's proper for others?

Once you have your basic needs met, and you know who you are and care about yourself, you don't need a lot of things to be happy. If you always need approval, you may have self-esteem issues that need to be addressed. Loving and accepting yourself as you are is the foundation of self-esteem, not in a narcissistic way but in a realistic way. Your self-concept is the most important aspect of your happiness and wellbeing.

Start to really love who you are. Not just some things about yourself, but everything—warts and all. There may be actions and behaviors we do not like about ourselves, but that doesn't mean we should dislike the whole of who we are. You want to become your own best friend. This won't happen overnight; it will take some time, but little steps will add up. Loving yourself is a lifelong commitment that never ends. You'll have rough spots in life, and your self-worth will be challenged, but if you have a strong foundation for self-esteem, you'll weather these storms.

You're probably thinking, "This is ridiculous. Of course, I care about myself." Think about it—if you really cared so much about yourself, would you be doing some of the things you're doing? Drinking, smoking, gambling, overworking, overspending, getting by with too little sleep? Would you be so critical of yourself and some of your behaviors? If we overdo any one activity, it could mean that deep down we don't really care about ourselves. It may be that you are trying to prove to yourself and to others that you have value. You want to treat yourself at least as good as you would treat others or your pet.

If you're engaged in any activity on a regular basis that's harmful to you, you don't love yourself. If you have peace of mind, all that external stimulation is not needed. It can be fun to have some of that stuff, but it's not necessary to be happy. When you feel better about yourself, you will find that a lot of the bad habits you've developed will fall by the wayside.

It's also important to eliminate any behaviors that can reduce your ability to love and accept yourself. If you're lying, cheating, holding resentment, or harboring jealousy of others, it will be extremely hard to accept yourself. These feelings will directly affect your self-esteem in a negative way. You must make feeling good about yourself a top priority, and that can be done only by eliminating destructive actions or thoughts. It is probably not possible to eradicate these actions and thoughts completely, but you can become more aware of them and work on changing them. This topic will be discussed further in the following chapters.

Nurturing yourself through self-love is a lifelong process, but it should get easier with time. If you can maintain self-love and self-acceptance, you will be able to resist the need for external things and situations to feel good about yourself. And if that external thing or event doesn't happen or suddenly ends, that's okay because it wasn't necessary to your life. It shouldn't shake you up too much because you already love and accept yourself exactly the way you are.

Another important way to increase your self-esteem is to realize that you have value and worth. You are just as worthy of occupying this planet as anyone else. If you are living your life believing you are less worthy than others, that needs to change. I cannot emphasize enough that your self-esteem is not based on what you're doing or accomplishing externally—it's totally based on how you feel about yourself as a person.

Being grateful for and enjoying what you have can improve your attitude. Being optimistic rather than pessimistic about life in general will also benefit your attitude. Be grateful for this time in your life. This is a God-given opportunity to be your authentic self. You may never have this incredible opportunity in life again. You no longer have to be someone you're not. You no longer have to present a facade to please your employer or clients. You have no more need to impress people.

It is hard to love ourselves or even like ourselves if we are not living our values. If you value good health but have allowed yourself to get out of shape, you probably aren't going to like your body too well, which can negatively affect your self-esteem. Taking steps, even small ones, toward reestablishing better health will raise your self-esteem. Doing nothing about it will make it hard for you to improve your negative feelings about yourself. Just starting the process of making things better can augment your self-esteem. As stated before, your values and beliefs may need to be updated. Some may be antiquated and harmful to your current life situation. If, as stated earlier, you value yourself only if you are gainfully employed and now you are retired, unless you change that belief, you would have to seek employment to raise your self-esteem.

Stick to your values and beliefs, but have a good handle on what they are and why they are important to you. If you have no idea what your values and beliefs are, start to work on discovering them. Books and websites can help with this self-discovery process. You are not the only one lacking knowledge in this area. If you don't examine the inconsistencies between your values, beliefs, actions, and behaviors, you will be directionless in the attempt to elevate your self-esteem. You might also be someone who knows his or her values and beliefs but is wishy-washy when it comes to applying them. When this happens, your self-esteem can decline, and it will not rise again unless the behavior, belief, or value changes. Here are two websites that can get you started with identifying some of your core values. The second has core beliefs information you can explore for yourself:

https://scottjeffrey.com/personal-core-values
www.pathwaytohappiness.com/writings_core_beliefs.htm

Make it a fun experience to learn about yourself. The self-discovery process can be fascinating and exciting once we commit to it.

"Rather than love, than money, than fame, give me truth."
— *Henry David Thoreau*

In summary, the best way to ensure healthy self-esteem is first and foremost to love and accept yourself for who you are and realize you are worthy. This means total love and acceptance, not conditional in any way. Stick to your values and live life with those values in mind. If you don't know what your values are, take the time to learn them. Constantly pay attention to your feelings and moods and how they pertain to your self-esteem. Don't wallow around waiting for something or someone to elevate your self-esteem; do it for yourself, now.

Throughout your life, loved ones and friends will come and go, but you will be there 100 percent of the time. You are the only person you can count on 1,440 minutes a day, 365 days a year for a lifetime. Living that intimately, for many years, with a person you don't like will seem like a long and arduous experience. Why not, instead, develop a good, strong, and positive relationship with that person?

Remember, applying the being RETIRED philosophy and raising your self-esteem leads to positive growth, resulting in less PMS symptoms. This leads to more positive growth, which improves your self-esteem, giving rise to still more positive growth, and the cycle continues until your attitude is airborne.

> "To be yourself in a world that is constantly trying to make you something else is the greatest accomplishment."
> — *Ralph Waldo Emerson*

### Questions for Reflection

1) How good is your self-esteem?

2) Are you a people pleaser?

3) Do you buy things to impress others?

4) Do you have behaviors that are harmful to your mind and body?

5) Take an online self-esteem assessment. Do the results surprise you?

6) Do you accept yourself fully?

## Chapter Six
## Your Mind Creates Your Reality

EVEN THOUGH I'M a doctor and have had many years of formal education, until I retired, I was ignorant of how large a role the mind plays in our lives. As I started reading more about living in the present and being mindful, I began paying more attention to my thoughts and my reactions to people and situations. I noticed that when I was more alert to what I was thinking, particularly when I was having negative thoughts, I became less critical of myself and others. Then I was happier because I was more accepting of people and situations. Consequently, I realized that our thoughts can directly affect our feelings and moods.

The power of our minds to make life wonderful or terrible is captured in a poem I like by British philosopher and inspirational writer James Allen (1864-1912).

### Mind

Mind is the master planner that molds and makes
And man is mind and forever more he takes,

The tools of thought and shaping what he wills
Brings forth a thousand joys, a thousand ills

He thinks in secret and it comes to pass
His environment is but his looking glass.

### *Pay Attention to Your Thoughts and Emotions*

Paying attention to your thoughts and feelings will help you to identify the cause of your unwanted moods. When I paid more attention to my thoughts, I noticed that they often involved some form of negativity. A lot of my thoughts were self-critical, being concerned with what I assumed other people were thinking about me and what I was lacking. Such thoughts made me feel anxious and unsettled. When I made attempts to be aware of and reframe them, my anxiety lessened. With time and effort, my negative thoughts became less intense and less frequent. This, of course, was all done in my mind.

The beliefs we have are based on our thoughts and how we feel about ourselves and life in general. At times, our thoughts are so strong and frequent that they become beliefs. From these beliefs will come thoughts and feelings about how things should be. If we believe people should work at jobs they hate until they physically can't do them anymore, then we'll have critical thoughts about ourselves when we retire. If we think we are inadequate, in some way, over time that will become a belief and we will act accordingly.

Changing your life for the better begins with changing outdated beliefs, and our beliefs are rooted in our thoughts. Your beliefs may have served you well during your career, but once you retire, they may be a detriment to your happiness.

"There is only one cause of unhappiness: the false beliefs you have in your head, beliefs so widespread, so commonly held, that it never occurs to you to questions them."
— *Anthony de Mello*

It is good to start identifying antiquated beliefs—the ones causing you unhappiness. Then you can work on changing them. If you believe no one respects you, that belief is most likely based in your belief that you don't deserve respect. There is no way you can know what people are thinking, and no one can plant thoughts in your head. So, when you feel nobody respects you, that feeling is self-generated. Once you identify these beliefs and thoughts, you can start changing them. Work on reframing your negative thoughts to put a more positive spin on them. The new belief might be that all people, including yourself, are deserving of respect. This would, hopefully, lead to treating yourself and others with respect and expecting to be treated respectfully by others.

The best way to identify our negative or antiquated beliefs is to pay attention to our moods, actions, and behaviors and then question why we feel or behave the way we do. For example, ask yourself questions such as:

- Why am I irritable?
- Why am I drinking more than usual?
- Why do I always need other people's approval?
- Why am I fatigued?
- Why am I gaining weight?
- What activities and people energize me and what activities and people deplete my energy?

In other words, get in touch with yourself. Questioning your feelings and actions when they are happening means you are right there in the moment. Let's say you are talking to someone and you suddenly feel angry; you can pause for a second and ask yourself why. You can then determine whether the anger is warranted and what to do about it. This way you are in touch with your thoughts and feelings. For example, I recall one time when I arrived early for a meeting, the secretary informed me that the chairman would not be there so I would have to chair the meeting. Upon hearing that, I felt my heart start to race and I started to sweat. I questioned, in my mind, why I felt that way—I had chaired numerous times before and knew everyone well. After I reminded myself that I was capable of the task and it shouldn't be a problem, my heart rate declined and my brow became less moist. Rather than get upset and bent out of shape, I could relax myself and chair the committee meeting. I am sure you can recall similar experiences of your own.

Some of us cannot relax and just be in the moment. We don't feel right unless we're engaged in some activity. In those situations, we're trying to outrun our thoughts and feelings. If we're constantly busy, then we don't have to face the difficult issues in our lives. Work often provided a nice hiding place from our problems and thoughts. Staying very busy in retirement can have the same affect.

Staying busy is a hard habit to break because it appears to have a beneficial effect, at least in the short-term. We may feel good because we're avoiding painful or bothersome issues. This type of action can go on for decades, and we can appear to be doing quite well. The problem often doesn't arise until there is a reason why we can't be busy, such as an illness or retirement. Then the time is available for our minds to take over.

Whether we want to believe it or not, there is a connection between the mind and body. How we perceive and think about ourselves and our problems always affects our actions and behaviors. If we are down on ourselves, then we're opening ourselves up for all sorts of physical and mental problems just like in the example I gave above when I felt I couldn't chair the meeting; my thoughts and perceptions sped up my heart, and then when I changed them, they slowed it down. Nothing outside of my mind and thoughts caused my heartbeat to accelerate and then decline. The sweating was brought on by the thoughts I was having about the situation. As soon as I was able to reassure myself of a safe and good outcome, I returned to normal. I am sure you can think of similar situations in your own life, although at the time you may not have realized you could change your thoughts and reaction.

I can't emphasize this enough: Pay attention to your feelings and behaviors—pay attention, pay attention, pay attention. Know thyself. If you've been neglecting introspection and self-reflection, start now. As an old adage says, "The best time to plant a tree is twenty years ago. The second-best time is today."

Another thing you can do is ask people who care about you whether you appear negative. We reflect our thoughts in our behavior and speech, so others will notice if we are negative. If you ask people and they think that's the case, work on changing your thoughts and beliefs.

Once you learn to recognize a change in mood, you may be able to trace it back to a particular thought. Paying attention to our thoughts and how they affect us allows us to nip unwanted moods in the bud. If we're always thinking negatively about ourselves and our lives, we're most likely to fall into a sad or melancholy mood. If unaddressed, most negative feelings get worse, so the melancholy can progress to depression and despair.

The opposite is also true—by having a more positive spin on life and more positive thoughts, we're likely to be more upbeat. This is not the same as positive thinking; it's more like reframing thoughts to alter their effect on your mood.

### Reframe Your Negative Thoughts into Positive Ones

Let's look at two examples of people who reframed their thoughts. The first person, Steve, in the examples is not real, but he serves to demonstrate how to use a positive spin approach to a difficult situation.

Steve just broke his leg, and it is going to take eight weeks to mend. During that time, he will have to remain at home. He won't be able to work or go anywhere.

His first take on this situation is: This is awful; my life is terrible. What will I do? What did I do to deserve this? This should have happened to my enemy Joe.

His second take, once he realizes he's being negative, could go like this: Okay I broke my leg. Well, this will be a new experience for me. I will learn what it is like to live with a broken leg and be dependent on others. Maybe I can reflect on my life? I will certainly have time to read the classics. I have always wanted to learn to play the harmonica. After all this, I am going to write a book to help others cope with a similar problem. I will be meeting a lot of new people like doctors, nurses, and physical therapists. I could possibly meet my future wife. Eight weeks isn't all that long, and I can handle it just like the many tough situations I have been in before.

For our second example, let's look again at my former patient, Mr. Smith, who was in a nursing home. How did he come to the conclusion that he was happy there? Perhaps his process went something like this.

First take: I have lost most things in life and now I have to give up my independence. Life isn't fair. I have nothing to live for. I might as well be dead.

Second take: I have had a great life. I had a beautiful wife and children. I had a career I enjoyed and many pleasurable possessions. I have noticed over the last couple of years that trying to keep up a house and do the maintenance has been getting harder. Going grocery shopping and preparing the food has been nearly impossible. Nobody visits me at home, so I feel lonely. What if I fell and was found dead? That would be so embarrassing. In the nursing home, I don't have to worry about those things. The food is good. I have people to talk to and can watch my sports on TV. Hopefully, if asked, I can pass on some wisdom from my many years of experience. I can be a role model on aging gracefully and give people empathy when needed. I am going to hire a ghost writer to write my memoir so I can leave a legacy and share what I have learned. Maybe I can even supplement my Social Security by playing Texas Hold'em with the staff? I am going to make the best of it and adjust my attitude. I can't wait to see my doctor to tell him how happy I am.

The first example concerned dealing with a health problem while the second was a situational issue. This practice can be applied to most problems in your life, even your retirement. Instead of concentrating on what you have lost or what is no longer present, you can put a positive spin on it. You can view retirement as a time of more freedom and self-discovery, not as if your life is ruined. Your thoughts might include: *Retirement is unchartered, but I am up for the task.*

The greatest thing about putting a positive spin on things is that it is totally controlled by you. It also helps you become more flexible and resilient (those two important qualities mentioned earlier) in handling the problems and changes you will run into in life. It can even help when you have big losses in your life. There is probably no greater loss than when a loved one dies, but a positive spin can even be applied there. This would be possible, however, only after a period of normal and needed grief. Nothing is all good or all bad. I am not trying to sugar-coat some of the tragedies we will face in life, but we can handle those tragedies better when we look at things from a positive angle.

"When you change your thoughts, you change your destiny."
— *Fortune Cookie*

Pay attention to your negative thoughts. Don't try to suppress them because they will return with greater intensity and frequency. Just pay attention and become aware of how often you're having them. That awareness will help you recognize patterns in the way you think, and you can then start reframing the negative thoughts into more positive ones.

The ability to recognize our negative thoughts and then reframe them in a positive way is invaluable for handling life's many challenges. For example, when you look back on problems you've had, you can reframe the thought by thinking about how the problem has made you a better person or the good that came out of the situation. Instead of thinking that your life has been a disaster because of some problem, try to think of yourself in a good regard. Remind yourself of your good qualities and your accomplishments. Become your own best friend and trust your intuition. These positive thoughts about yourself can have a big impact on how your life goes.

It's important to learn how to direct our minds by dealing with our thoughts effectively. We can use our mind to create and solve problems, but the mind will create problems if not trained. If we let our thoughts go wild, we can create all kinds of distressing feelings. Our thoughts can drive us crazy, and most people who are depressed and anxious are in those states because of their denigrating thoughts. If we're under stress, we're more apt to have unpleasant thoughts. It takes time and practice, but we can learn to acknowledge and reframe them.

### Create Positive Coping Skills by Replacing the Negative Ones

Throughout life, we're faced with trying situations. We may have had a rough childhood, experienced tough times in school, or faced other events that caused us stress. During these stressful times, we developed coping skills or strategies; some were helpful, but some were harmful.

The coping strategies that helped us withstand and endure stress throughout our lives, including at work, will be the same ones available to us during retirement. If we've used negative strategies, such as drinking alcohol, watching TV excessively, or gambling, those actions will lead to negative growth and will delay or halt our progression through the retirement transition stages.

When we engage in activities that impede our growth, greater negativity can be generated in the form of negative feelings about ourselves because we are doing activities inconsistent with our values. It is hard to produce positive thoughts when, deep down, you don't feel positive about your actions. These coping strategies will compromise your relationship with yourself and also affect your relationships with other people. In a sense, you're stifling your progress and sabotaging any chance for a happy, successful retirement. These actions will certainly have a negative impact on your retirement.

While negative coping mechanisms preclude progress and positive growth, healthy ways of coping can make the transition shorter and less burdensome. Healthy coping strategies would include an exercise routine, supportive relationships, hobbies, and relaxation techniques. If you haven't developed these strategies prior to your retirement, then it should be a priority to institute them as soon as possible. Doing so will pay dividends because your wellbeing will improve and you will create a smoother path to retirement. You are then creating an environment in your mind for more positivity.

Retirement can last a very long time and require a lot of coping skills. You'll have a lot of time on your hands to engage in unhealthy behaviors if you choose to do so. If you're inclined to drink when under stress, you'll have a lot more time to drink. The same goes for other non-beneficial activities. It's important to recognize how we cope with stress and to replace the harmful coping mechanisms with healthier ones.

### Learn How to Maintain a Good Attitude

We can all agree that a good attitude is essential to an enjoyable retirement. Hopefully, we also agree that our attitude is under our control. Achieving a favorable attitude is an ongoing endeavor, something you have to work on every day for the rest of your life. It may seem like a lot of hard work, but it's just a matter of changing your thinking. Monitoring your thoughts and feelings will be a lifelong process that becomes natural over time.

Living in the present as much as possible will greatly improve your attitude. It takes time and practice to learn to live in the present, but it is necessary for happiness and peace of mind. True happiness can only happen in the present moment. When you are wholly in the present, you have no regrets about the past or anxieties about the future.

Prescription for a Happy Retirement 71

These changes will not happen quickly. Some people work on developing these skills their whole lives, but they still don't master them. You owe it to yourself to work on developing them.

Our attitudes will change as situations in life change. People can be inconsistent in their feelings and actions toward us. Situations in life can change very fast, throwing us into chaos. But if we consistently accept, love, and respect ourselves, it will be easier for us to adjust our thoughts to the positive. If we become dependent on other people, possessions, or events to elevate our self-esteem and attitude, we'll always be on an emotional roller coaster. Then it will be more difficult to put a positive spin on negative events. But if we can approach things more positively, and we are consistent, we can handle life's ups and downs.

If you can view your life as a journey and every day as an adventure, you're more apt to enjoy the process and not just the destination. Knowing that you're capable of dealing with the changes that occur throughout life will build your self-confidence. Avoiding or resisting change will only lead to suffering. It's best to accept change and adapt to whatever it brings. People who remain flexible by putting a positive spin on their thinking and actions are much happier.

You may have been wronged by someone in the past, but you damage yourself by keeping it in your thoughts. You don't have to forget what happened, but it's best to forgive and search for some positive outcome that may have resulted. You can choose to give up those non-productive thoughts and replace them with beneficial thoughts. If you accept yourself totally and unconditionally, things that upset you in the past will bother you less. When someone does you wrong, it speaks more of that person's character than yours. Try not to take things personally and don't get easily offended.

It's unrealistic to expect that you'll have a positive attitude all the time. We all have periods of change in our lives that require time to adjust and adapt, so if you're feeling useless, irrelevant, or lonely, remember that these are just thoughts in your mind. You're creating those feelings through thoughts, so you can replace them with better thoughts. If you are experiencing extreme difficulty during times of change, and that is causing quality of life issues, you may consider seeking professional assistance. However, most issues can be dealt with effectively through thought adjustment.

I'm convinced that some people actually get addicted to negative thinking. Start working on your awareness of your thought patterns and then work on reframing your thoughts. Don't allow yourself to be stuck in this negative stance. Instead, recognize and reframe. Reframing is a major thing we can do to improve our attitudes. Distracting ourselves from negative thinking may be effective in the short-term, but those negative thoughts will eventually return with a vengeance and be more difficult to extinguish.

### *The Benefits of Cognitive Behavioral Therapy*

Instead of mastering our thoughts and minds, too many of us turn to distractions to numb ourselves or avoid pain. This approach can backfire and cause you to feel much worse when distractions aren't available. You will then be totally unprepared to face major changes in your life. If one of our distractions involves a chemical substance, we may end up with an addiction in addition to the underlying problem we are trying to avoid. Awareness is the key because it starts the process of self-discovery. If you're unaware of your negative thoughts, and the feelings and emotions associated with them, you'll never be able to improve your attitude.

No one else can come to your rescue because this is your issue. They can only guide you. Your thoughts are yours alone, and only you can reframe them to reverse their negativity. These negative thoughts, as we discussed earlier, are a major factor in why we become melancholic during retirement. Sometimes medication can help in the short-term, but it doesn't teach us the skills we need to manage the thoughts. It will just mask the melancholy with a better mood; once the medication is stopped, the melancholy will most likely return, especially if you didn't work on your thought management while on the medication.

In most cases, PMS doesn't require medication to be treated; it can be improved with thought awareness and management. Many therapists specialize in Cognitive Behavioral Therapy (CBT), which helps people work with and challenge their thoughts. The CBT approach can be very helpful because it teaches you to become your own therapist. People are taught how to recognize their improper thinking and how to alter thoughts in a way that will better their lives. If you're a person who works best with someone instructing you and giving you feedback, CBT would be a good way to go.

I think most people with PMS can achieve good results on their own, but it's also good to know that help is available if needed. Because PMS is a problem having to do with loss, it's to your benefit to learn better ways of dealing with loss, which then can be applied to new losses when they occur. We will never completely master our thoughts, but reframing even a small percentage of them can be of benefit. Work on reframing your thoughts every day, and in time, you'll become more adept at it. The main thing is repetition and sticking with it. Reframing is not trying to trick yourself into thinking everything is rosy. It is more about looking at both sides of any situation and realizing the potential good that can result.

Of course, some of the problems that people have are beyond the scope of this type of action. You may need to consult a specialist if your problems exceed your ability to deal with them. That said, I have seen people put a positive spin on situations that most people would think to be impossible. I have had many patients say that illnesses or accidents changed their lives for the better. As funny as it may seem, these people looked at their illnesses or injuries as blessings. Some have even looked for and found the humor in their situations. Dr. Ben Carson changed his life, for the better, after being diagnosed with prostate cancer. It was a signal that he needed to change his diet, reduce his stress, and spend more time with his family. He didn't look at it as a disaster but as a beneficial event. It's possible that some people might have had shorter lives if it were not for the life-threatening diagnoses they had. I had a professor who swore his diabetes made him feel healthier because it forced him to lose weight and to exercise.

### *Keep a Journal*

Writing down your thoughts and feelings can be a great way to become aware of how they affect your mood. You'll become much more cognizant of the negative thoughts you're having about yourself and your situation. You'll see in print how your thinking plays such an important part in how you feel. You can then reframe your thoughts and feelings into a more positive light.

Keeping a journal or writing down your feelings is like discussing your problems with a friend and bouncing ideas off someone you trust. After all, you should be your own best friend, right? Only you know about the experiences you've been through and how you handled challenges in the past. You can write anything you want, analyze it, reframe it, and then destroy it if you so desire.

I suggest writing at the end of the day. Write about what went on, your thoughts and feelings, and what you did to improve how you were feeling. Then congratulate yourself for working on gaining insight into some of your thoughts and behaviors. Over time, writing should become a habit, and you'll become aware of your thoughts more readily even when not writing about them. You can then reframe those thoughts.

Before I started keeping a journal, I never would have believed that writing things down could be beneficial, but it really does help. After all, our attitudes and actions are directly related to what we're thinking and to our underlying beliefs. If our thoughts, beliefs, and actions are in harmony, we will have a positive attitude; if not, our attitude will be poor.

Again, if you believe retired people are lazy, then you'll view yourself as lazy when retired. Examining this underlying belief and changing how you think about this issue will improve your attitude. Remember: Our thoughts are not reality; they are merely chemical reactions taking place in our nervous system. Just because we think something doesn't mean it is true or that it will become a reality. We have to keep our thoughts and beliefs in perspective, and realize that we have assumptions and biases based on our experiences and backgrounds. Over the years, we have collected a lot of dogma that doesn't serve much purpose for us today. Evaluating the accuracy of our beliefs and thoughts, and then changing them as necessary, can improve our outlook. Using the positive spin will go a long way toward improving our quality of life as well. It's worth the effort to develop a more positive regard to the situations we face.

In summary, living the being RETIRED philosophy, increasing your self-esteem, and putting a positive spin on life leads to positive growth. Positive growth results in continued improvement of your PMS symptoms, which allows further positive growth to occur, and the circle continues. Your attitude is climbing as a result of these practices.

## Questions for Reflection

1) Are you aware of your thought patterns?

2) Do you look on the bright side of things, or are you more negative?

3) Can you identify any strong beliefs that would hamper a happy retirement?

4) How have you formed your beliefs?

5) Do you hold onto thoughts about bad experiences?

6) Try putting a positive spin on a negative experience from your past. For example, if you lost your job, could you put a positive spin on that situation by finding the good that resulted from it?

R̥

## Chapter Seven
# A Few Core Principles for Emotional Health

A s I'VE DISCUSSED earlier, retirement may be the biggest change we have to deal with in life. No matter who you are or what your situation is, there will be an adjustment phase. It's normal to go through a grieving period that can last several months or longer. It's normal to have a period of disenchantment and discomfort after you retire. You've made a major change in your life, and that mustn't be taken lightly.

Throughout this book, I have implied that prolonged disillusionment and PMS are the same and can have a deleterious effect on a person's retirement. As I have stated earlier, disillusionment is a normal stage of retirement and can be beneficial and worked through. Post-Work Melancholy Syndrome is a syndrome I invented for those not coming out of the disillusioned stage, and who don't realize that PMS is what is negatively affecting their quality of life. Ideally, a person would advance through the disillusioned stage without consequence. But prolonged disillusionment or PMS can potentially derail the normal progression through the stages of retirement. If the disillusionment and/or melancholy are serving the purpose of getting the retiree to act, then it is beneficial. By referring to the disillusionment as "prolonged," I mean that the stage is "no longer useful." It is not serving any purpose. Feelings of disillusionment or melancholy are not bad unless they are arresting your growth and the changes you need to make.

A normal or usual length of time for the stage of disillusionment can't be determined because it will vary from person to person. It occurs when a person is not satisfied with his life or not happy with the way things are going. If these feeling are giving you the impetus to change your life for the better, they can be of great service. If they are not, or, in fact, they are decreasing the quality of your life, then they are counterproductive and possibly very harmful. So, a period that is "prolonged" could begin after weeks or months, depending on whether the disenchanted feeling is helping you to take the initiative to grow or it is impeding your progress.

It might be easier to understand what I mean by prolonged disillusionment or PMS through an illustration using people as an example. Let's take three individuals (Mary, Gary, and Terry) who retired on the same day and are roughly the same age. During her working years, Mary had developed many interests and activities outside of her job. After retiring from work, she felt disillusioned for a few short weeks, but her quality of life was unaffected. She continued with the same relationships and interests that she had before retiring, and within a few months, Mary was very happy with her life. Mary breezed through the disillusioned stage, which is not typical of most retirees. Gary hadn't prepared as well for retirement. He entered the disillusioned stage blindly and wasn't sure what to do. He knew the feelings of disappointment and sadness were normal, but he also realized that he didn't want to continue in his current state of mind. After a few months, he decided to act—to find out what he could do to change his life for the better. As soon as he started doing things to improve his situation, the disappointed and sad feelings started to subside. Gary did not suffer from prolonged disillusion or PMS, and if he did, it served to benefit him overall. Gary realized his plight and did what he needed to do to change his feelings. This again is not that common with retirees. Terry, on the other hand, was totally unprepared for retirement. She went into the disillusioned stage and felt sad and disappointed most of the time. She began filling her time with uninspiring things like gambling and watching TV. When she was involved in these activities, she didn't notice the disappointed and sad feelings, but when she was not occupied, the feelings were intense. She was not satisfied with her life, and she was filling up her days with activities just to keep busy. Over time, she became more irritable and her quality of life was being affected. She knew she wasn't happy or satisfied with her life, but she couldn't put her finger on why. On the outside, she appeared to be functioning well, and other people hadn't noticed any major changes in her behavior. Terry was suffering from prolonged disillusionment or PMS, and, unfortunately, many people have a retirement experience similar too Terry's. It doesn't matter whether Terry was disillusioned for a few weeks or many months; it was prolonged and it was negatively affecting her quality of life. So, even though it is normal to go through a disillusioned stage in retirement, it is not usual for it to disrupt the quality and satisfaction of a person's life. It can have a happy ending though, like Terry had. Terry ran into Bill, an old friend, when she stopped for gas on her way to the casino. He recognized that Terry was suffering from Post-Work Melancholy Syndrome since he himself had suffered from it just a few months previously. He loaned her his copy of *Prescription for a Happy Retirement*. She read it, applied the principles, and got involved in new interests. She noticed her attitude improve, and she was happier. When she went over to Bill's to thank him and return the book, Bill proposed marriage. I heard they are now living in a remote mining town somewhere in the Keweenaw Peninsula. Good things happen with the right attitude.

The problem is when people get stuck in feelings of sadness and melancholy and don't recognize it as an indication that change is necessary. It is not evident to them that their minds are telling them growth and adaptation are needed. As a result, they may continue to spiral down and become depressed. I'm sure we all know of people who fit this description; we may even feel this way ourselves.

The whole point of this book is to help you through the transition stages of retirement, from initial disenchantment, to reorientation, and then to a happy, healthy retirement. The goal is to not get stuck in the disenchantment, but to move on to developing and accepting the new life you are creating.

It's my view that people who get stuck in disenchantment or become melancholic are not experiencing those feelings because they miss their jobs. Up to 70 percent of working people don't like their jobs. Unless you were in the lucky 30 percent, you're probably not missing your job that much.

Nevertheless, I've heard people say, "I was a lot happier when I was working." Really? Again, the issue is not missing the job—it's missing the *feeling* you derived from doing the activity associated with the work. So, adjusting to retirement means adjusting to the loss of that feeling.

There are four ways you can make that adjustment:

1. Do nothing and continue to feel disillusioned, sad, and melancholic. This is the easiest choice, but not one I would recommend.

2. Beg for your job back and hope that works. This is unlikely to occur, and if it does, your skills may not be up to par because of how long you've been away.

3. Find a different but similar situation that would provide you with the same feelings that work provided, like starting your own business or doing volunteer work. This would probably be okay and is what most retirement books would recommend. But what happens if the situation doesn't work out? You're then back to square one and the melancholy.

4. Separate your happiness from the feelings you derived from your work. Remember that feelings come from thoughts, so changing your thoughts should result in a change in feelings. It's that simple, but it's not easy to do.

### *Build a Strong Foundation on a Few Core Principles*

This is by far the longest chapter in this book and possibly the most important. It expounds on some of the issues we have already addressed and delves into other areas. In my opinion, it would be extremely difficult or impossible to have happiness in your retirement without instituting the ideas brought up in this chapter. Recognizing the negativity around us and inside of us is necessary so we can work on eliminating it. We can't do this without looking deep into how we view life.

In order to have the proper groundwork for a great retirement, you must take good care of yourself. Become your own best friend, and make happiness one of your purposes in life. Happiness is contagious and can be shared, so by increasing and maintaining your happiness, you're benefiting yourself and society. It's a win-win situation. You can't expect to be happy all the time, but with self-knowledge, you can increase the happy times and reduce the sad ones. But first we need to look at how we can reduce negativity to make room for the happiness.

To develop and maintain a good attitude, you have to put down a strong foundation based on a few core principles. In this chapter, we'll look at core principles and approaches for achieving and maintaining emotional health in retirement.

## *Gain Self-Knowledge*

As far back as ancient Greece, people knew the importance of knowing thyself. This is the greatest gift you can give yourself. Instead of our emotions getting the best of us, we can work to use our emotions to our benefit.

Most of us haven't taken the time to really get to know ourselves and become our own best friends. I'm certainly guilty of that. We can get away with not knowing ourselves as long as life is going well and we're distracted. It's when we have problems or a crisis that knowing ourselves is the most needed.

Knowing how we react to and cope with difficult situations can help us solve problems in better ways when they arise. We are also then more apt to know our weaknesses and vulnerabilities so we can avoid those things that cause us suffering. Having a true love of ourselves can help when adversity strikes because we'll still love ourselves no matter what. When we lack self-knowledge and love for ourselves, we're set up for problems. We're more likely to be self-critical and put ourselves down when things go wrong. We are more apt to fall prey to scams and disingenuous people. Mental and physical illnesses are much more common in people who are not living their values. But first, you have to know what those values are by doing the internal work necessary to identify them.

As I've mentioned several times now, most bad habits are a symptom of something deeper going on. The need to address the underlying problems cannot be overemphasized. The underlying problems will not magically go away when you retire. In fact, if not addressed, they may come crashing in on you.

If you've become dependent on certain habits to distract you from what is going on in your life, you've been avoiding the root problem. If you can determine why you engage in certain habits, you can work on getting to the problem's source.

Without self-knowledge, our ways of coping may do more harm than good. If we care about ourselves, we're more likely to treat ourselves with kindness, understanding, and forgiveness. We'll cope with problems in more constructive ways. Treating ourselves lovingly will help us to become more resilient to life's downers. If you know your strengths and weaknesses, you can avoid certain situations or work on developing the skills to adjust. You may be feeling bad and negative, but you don't know why, so you start drinking or engaging in some other bad behavior, which only makes the matter worse.

We all have to do what's right for ourselves, and no one can determine what's best for you or me. It's good to trust ourselves, but first, we must learn about ourselves and what makes our lives enjoyable. This takes time and effort, but it is well worth it. Self-discovery can result in many beneficial consequences. In a sense, this entire book is about the value of self-discovery and self-knowledge.

Since I retired, I have devoted a lot of time to determining why I felt the need to be busy all the time. Through persistence, I have been able to unearth the most probable cause. I still feel the need to stay busy, but with this self-knowledge, I can address the root cause and change the behavior. Without this newfound awareness, it would be much harder to enjoy my life. Start to question your behaviors. Dig deep into knowing the reasons for them.

### Remove Negativity from Your Life

We have talked about removing negative thoughts, but that's only part of it. You must remove negativity from your life. In the last chapter, we discussed putting a positive spin on negative experiences and thoughts, but sometimes you can't put a positive spin on them, especially when it comes to dealing with negative people, situations, experiences, and behaviors. As time goes on, we may become more cynical about our lives and situations. We may become negative about things without even realizing it. If you're having mostly negative thoughts, your behaviors will reflect it and people will mirror this negativity back to you, so that it can become a never-ending cycle. As previously mentioned, some people become addicted to this negative feeling and it becomes chronic. The smart ones will pick up on your negativity and start avoiding you. Negativity is like a cancer that feeds on you, leading to all kinds of problems. Cynicism needs to be eliminated because you can't just put a positive spin on it. Become aware of when you seem cynical, and work on not allowing it to affect your mood.

Don't waste your time criticizing yourself and others—it can lead to unhappiness. Have you ever seen a happy person who's very critical? Being critical, in particular situations, to bring about a change can be beneficial, but having an ongoing critical nature benefits no one. It also causes negative thoughts and feelings. Avoid comparing yourself to others or to your former self. It's not fair to compare the best parts of others with your not-so-great parts; that will only lead to feelings of inferiority. Being negative and exposing yourself to a lot of negativity during your retirement will definitely spoil your efforts to resolve PMS.

Once you learn to recognize negativity in your thoughts and attitude, it will become less of a problem. I remember when a patient once phoned me to thank me for something I had done. She was extremely appreciative, and it sure felt good to hear it. Within a half hour, I got another phone call from a patient who was very upset that I hadn't filled out his insurance form. Needless to say, my good mood disappeared almost instantly. I got busy and finished the form, but that encounter bothered me for several hours. Had I put more emphasis on the first situation, I would have saved myself some grief. Yes, I know it would have been best to have finished the form on time, but I hope you get the picture. If we focus more on the negative aspects of our lives, it will directly influence how we feel.

Our feelings and moods are dependent on what we feed our minds. When we think good thoughts, our moods will be better. We can put a positive spin on some negative thoughts, as we discussed in the last chapter, but some thoughts and situations have to be stopped entirely. We will discuss these further throughout this chapter.

Avoid toxic people, places, and situations. These include anything that's going to bring you down: family, friends, relationships, food, and social media. We discussed negative people in Chapter Four, but some people will drain the positive energy right out of us. It's like they attach a siphon hose to you and you can feel your zest for life being removed. It is almost as if you had a quart of blood removed but are still expected to function normally.

Certain people with personality disorders prey on people's emotions and can wreak distress on the unwary. Pay attention to how you feel when you encounter these people, and either limit your time with them or avoid the ones who drain you dry. I noticed right away that some people had that effect on me, but I couldn't explain why. When we are struggling with self-esteem issues and lack confidence, we are more inclined to tolerate negative behavior from others. As we start adjusting to retirement and become more self-educated, our tolerance for those people will be much less. Awareness, again, is the key, and remember, it is not your job to make others happy and cheerful. That is up to them.

The food we eat can affect the way we feel. If we are eating a lot of garbage foods, our moods will generally be down. Treat your body well by avoiding foods that are not good for you. Also avoid toxic substances like alcohol, which is a poison and can cause physical and psychological damage to the body. Many recreational drugs are depressants, so if you are already feeling down, they can make the situation worse. Also, when we are feeling down, our chance for addiction increases.

Next, never gossip about or judge others; doing so will not make you any better and only increases negativity. As they say, "If a person gossips with you, they will gossip about you." Gossip is a way of boosting ourselves up at the expense of someone else. It is not mentally healthy, and it can be energy draining. Once you start working on the no gossip rule, you will be much better at realizing when others do it. When we hear gossip, our views become tainted so that the person being gossiped about is not given a fair shake. When you stop gossiping and listening to gossip, you feel a whole lot lighter. When we don't feel good about ourselves, we are more likely to mistreat others. Our behaviors are many times just a reflection of how we feel about ourselves. Always try to be kind to people and treat them with respect. Then they will be more inclined to treat you the same.

When we feel bad about ourselves, we sometimes compensate by overdoing or overachieving. This can backfire on us if we are unable to meet our expectations or don't enjoy the activity by only making us feel worse. This result will make you feel negative and unworthy. Stop trying to keep accomplishing more and more. You don't need to keep proving yourself to anyone, including yourself. Start doing things for the enjoyment and the experience of them, and not so you have something to brag about. Doing the things you truly enjoy will bring many positives to your life both socially and health-wise. Removing the stress-inducing activities we overdo just to feel good about ourselves makes room for the positive activities we could be experiencing.

Over the years, we may have displaced our sense of humor and begun looking at the dark side of everything. If so, we need a reality check because this state of mind can put us in negative territory. It's hard to do, but try to stop taking yourself so seriously. Start to lighten up—life is short, so enjoy it. After years of raising a family, trying to meet deadlines, and dealing with all of life's issues, we may have lost our zest for life. Begin looking at the humorous side of life and have a good laugh at some of the bumps you've run into. Learn to laugh at yourself occasionally.

"You grow up the day you have your first good laugh at yourself."
— *Ethel Barrymore*

Many of us are perfectionists in some aspect of our lives. Perfectionism is equivalent to self-torture and cannot be sustained. You were never perfect and never will be, and neither will anybody else. Stop trying to be perfect and stop expecting life in retirement to be perfect. We are only setting ourselves up for disappointment if we expect perfection. Go with the flow as much as possible. If we have been perfectionists during our working years, now is the time to change. Perfectionism leads to worry and stress. You're putting unnecessary pressure on yourself, resulting in a less than enjoyable life. By pursuing perfection, you're playing a losing game and attracting negativity into your life.

In summary, the best and most effective way of eliminating negativity is first to become aware of it and then change it by creating a satisfying and enjoyable life. Start appreciating all the good you already have. Try to put a positive spin on what you can, but be willing to remove what you perceive to be negative and harmful to your wellbeing. Nothing is all good or all bad.

## *Judge Not*

A lot of our negativity comes from our feelings about ourselves and other people. We may not like someone and that person may be less than enthusiastic about us, but that doesn't mean we have to put him or her down, even if it is just in our minds. A major roadblock to an enjoyable retirement is judging people and feeling that you're being judged by others.

We may assume that people have a negative opinion of us and are critical of our way of life. But unless you have supernatural powers, there's no way you can know what people are thinking about you. Your feeling of being judged by others is more about how you feel deep down about yourself.

If you judge people unfairly, you are holding yourself to a higher standard. Let's say you judge a retired person as lazy. What happens when you retire? Do you suddenly change your judgment? Whatever is going on with others, which makes us we feel the need to judge, could happen to us.

It's unlikely that many people are all that concerned about you and your life decisions, so be less concerned about theirs.

If people do judge you, it's due to their own belief systems, which are totally independent from your beliefs. How does anyone know what's right for someone else? Other people don't know what you want out of life, and they haven't had the same experiences you or I have had. All of us experience life only once, so how can someone be an expert on the best way to live?

Don't get bogged down in worry about what others might think; most people have a hard time figuring out what's best for themselves. The knowledgeable people will accept you for who you are and what you're doing with your life. You can expect some criticism if you're doing something harmful to yourself or others, but if you're not doing anything unlawful or immoral, it's nobody's business. If someone with experience gives you constructive criticism, you may want to take a serious look at it; if there is merit in what they say, we can learn from it and possibly change some behavior. There are exceptions, but overall, don't let other people—or your thoughts about other people and what their thoughts about you might be—control what you think or do for yourself.

"Those who mind don't matter, and those who matter don't mind."
— *Bernard Baruch*

When we think people are being judgmental, it's mostly in our own minds and we're being overly critical about ourselves. By becoming aware of these inaccurate and critical thoughts and feelings, we can work on eliminating them. We also need to stop judging others in this way because that will lead us to judging ourselves. If we're more accepting of ourselves, we'll be more accepting of others.

Pay close attention to your thoughts about other people and try to work on reducing your critical judgments. This process is not easy and will take a lot of time, but it will be well worth it. You cannot have an enjoyable retirement if you're always worrying about being judged or judging people in a critical fashion. This is your journey, so you're entitled to live it the way you see fit, but I guarantee that eliminating the negativity will make it more enjoyable for you.

### Be Aware That Problems May Be There Before Retirement

If you're not happy before you retire, you're not likely to be happy after you retire. While you're still working, you can try to figure out where you're not happy and try to do something about it. If your home life is less than optimal, now is the time to resolve any major issues. Avoiding aspects of your life that need attention will only cause more problems down the road.

For many people, work is a distraction from life's problems and unresolved issues. Most people don't realize this; they just keep working, oblivious to the potential consequences. If we suffer from anxiety or depression, we may use work to avoid dealing with these feelings. Anxious or depressing thoughts can be suppressed if we're totally absorbed in our work, and the harder we work, the more those thoughts and feelings are suppressed. Even if this suppression goes on for years or even decades and we do reasonably well, ultimately, it is only a temporary fix. Eventually, the piper has to be paid. Work on the underlying problem, whether it is depression or anxiety, because just putting a positive spin on it is not enough.

Work can increase our adrenaline levels, which can mask symptoms of depression. If we keep working and suppressing our feelings, physical problems may start to appear—high blood pressure, insomnia, mood swings, and a range of other illnesses. Most people will not associate these symptoms with depression, so they will fail to change anything in their lives.

The real problem arises when people are no longer working because the suppressant is no longer there. Years of suppressing these feelings significantly magnifies their effects. It's like water building up behind a dam: when it lets loose, the feelings can be overwhelming and uncontrollable. At that point, long-suppressed thoughts and feelings will surface with a vengeance. Then the retired person doesn't know what hit him. He is depressed, but doesn't know why. The adrenaline is no longer at the level it was when he was working, so the symptoms of depression manifest.

One of the major reasons some people fail at retirement is because they can't deal with uncomfortable feelings of depression or anxiety; they then either rush back to some form of work, or they seek out another form of distraction. However, if we're aware that work can mask underlying psychological problems, we can begin to address them.

Once you know the cause of a problem, you can direct your energy toward resolving it. Finding the underlying reason for your anxiety or depression is the key; it is crucial for having an enjoyable retirement.

### Something Is Missing—Possibly Structure

In retirement, we can sometimes feel like something is missing. That's because something *is* missing. It's important to be aware of this feeling and not ignore it. The feeling is not necessarily a bad thing, although it may feel like it is. It can actually be a very good thing if used properly.

If you're unhappy and not enjoying your life, it's your mind's way of alerting you to the need to make some changes. It takes time and work to identify what needs to change and to work on it. But something important is missing, and you will not feel better until you find out what it is. If we ignore this feeling, it will cause us much negativity, not only for ourselves but also the people we have relationships with. This feeling is the same as the disenchanted and PMS feelings we may have.

Discovering what we need to replace or create can be an eye-opening experience and add to positive growth. It may be as simple as putting structure back into our lives.

Sometimes we feel as though we're all dressed up with no place to go. When we were working, our time was structured and we knew what was expected of us. In retirement, we have an abundance of unstructured time, and if we haven't dealt with unstructured time for many years, we may feel lost. Other people seem to have places to go and things they need to do. You may feel like you are in a different world. It's a little like when you were a kid on summer vacation. When school was out, you had to come up with your own plans and entertainment.

Retirement is a time when you can structure your own time or you can live unstructured. You can be like a musician who plays music according to the written score or you can write your own music and improvise. Some people, once they leave work, don't want any structure while others need to have a set schedule. It is up to you to determine what is best for you. I find that the combination of a little structure and no structure works the best for me. My mornings are very structured, but my afternoons are open for whatever. Seek out what could be missing in your life. Some structure in your life can be positive by giving you something to look forward to and be committed to.

### I'm Bored Out of My Gourd

A common complaint of retirees is being bored, of having nothing worthwhile to do. Boredom is a state of mind resulting from the feeling of having to be entertained. If this mindset is not altered, a lot of negativity can result, most likely in the form of a lack of motivation and inactivity. In retirement, there is a lot of time to fill, and it's impossible to be entertained and active every minute. When we're working at a job, our days are filled with stimulating activities, and when we get home, we have family activities to occupy the time. We're tired by the end of the day and just want to relax and be entertained by TV. When you're retired, you have at least eight hours a day, previously taken up by work, that now must be accounted for. It's very easy to feel like you've got no place to go and all day to get there.

If you've had trouble in the past with uncommitted time, this feeling of disorganization can be trying. Some of us will immediately attempt to reactivate our lives by getting involved in activities just to be busy. Others will fall prey to negative behaviors to reduce the anxiety of having too much time and nothing to do. People who have developed other interests and friends outside of work will do better with the change in lifestyle. It's good to have hobbies that involve some form of mental work, but boredom can also be a signal that you need to be creative and learn something new. It can mean that you need to begin searching for new interests and activities. This boredom doesn't mean you sit and wait for something to happen; it is a cue that action is needed. Doing nothing will result in a negative experience, but searching for and finding a new interest can be very positive.

### *The Inability to Spend Time Alone and Find New Interests*

Retirement may be the first time in our lives when we have to spend time alone. This situation can be frightening for a lot of reasons. Some of us just don't feel comfortable without others around. It may be a personality thing, but the odds are good that you will spend some time in your life alone. Having to spend time alone, when you are not used to it, can be a negative experience.

Some people have never spent time alone. They have gone from being with their family of origin to marriage, and have always had others around them. This may not be good in the long run because, as we age and family members die or move away, the odds are great that we will be alone sometime in our lives. It is good to develop the ability to be comfortable being alone for those reasons, but it also affords the opportunity to get to know ourselves better. Start to spend time alone and get used to it. This will help you to deal with the times when you are forced to be alone. You may find that you enjoy your own company and realize that it can have a positive effect on your life. There is a difference between being alone and being lonely.

Retirement can be a great opportunity to develop the capacity to spend time alone. We can discover activities that interest us and learn new things. Getting to know ourselves and learning how to use time wisely can be invaluable. You can read, exercise, meditate, or get involved in a hobby.

We lose inspiration and creativity when we're preoccupied with work; retirement is the time to reclaim that inspiration and creativity.

The options are limitless, but it may take a while to determine what's best for you.

## *Occupying Your Time*

When you're still working is the time to start thinking about how you want to spend your post-work time. Start carving out time to contemplate the things you're interested in. I believe most people are working to pay the bills or support a lifestyle, but there are probably a lot of other things they'd rather be doing. It might not be evident to you right now, but with a little effort, it's likely you'll find many interests and passions.

Not taking the time to do this while you're working will make it much harder to do later on. It does take motivation on your part. Otherwise, once you retire, just watching the clock tick off the minutes will be a negative experience.

You're probably getting the picture now that retirement is an active process. Doing it right takes introspection, planning, and action. Without ideas of what you want out of retirement, you will have no direction. These ideas must be your own and generated by you. After many years of meeting other people's expectations, you can finally be the architect of your life.

Don't waste the opportunity to plan for your retirement before you retire. We all know that plans don't always turn out like we would have wished, but if they do, you'll be prepared. If they don't, you'll at least be in a better position to come up with alternatives.

## *Learn to Be Patient and to Give Up Control*

They don't call patience a virtue for nothing. Retirement will be a negative experience if you don't have patience, so you must work on learning it. Patience is necessary in retirement because life will be unfolding at a different pace. When you're working, you may have more control over the events in your life, at least at work. When you're retired, the people you interact with will have their own agendas. You may have gotten used to giving orders and having someone immediately carry them out. This will be a rare situation in retirement. No one will jump to comply with your wishes.

If you got preferential treatment while you were working, that will most likely end in retirement. You may get special treatment occasionally, but don't expect it. If you retire in the town where you were employed, some people may remember you and roll out the red carpet, but most will not. If you retire to a town where people don't know you, be aware that you'll not be special. This can be a letdown if you're unprepared for it.

Patience is also needed to let things happen in the way they're intended to. It's good to let things evolve and not try to control the outcome. Nothing is going to happen overnight. Be patient with loved ones and the people you meet. They may be on a different wavelength than you and have different priorities. It's tough to develop patience, and some people never do, but it's well worth trying. This is character-building. If you are impatient by nature, start working on developing patience now. In retirement, you don't have to be rushing and all stressed out. You can give yourself leeway time for appointments and schedule commitments based on what works for you. Expect that things may not go as you had hoped, but try to be flexible and calm.

If you're able to go with the flow, you'll be better in all aspects of life. Let's say, for example, you develop a health condition that requires recovery. If you're not patient, understanding, and able to go with the flow, your recovery may be prolonged or result in further problems. Don't rush the process. Take it as it comes. A need to be in control all the time will have negative consequences on your retirement. Easing back on the controls will definitely help bring about a more positive retirement experience.

## Don't Make Your Happiness Conditional

One of the reasons people aren't happy when they retire is because they've pulled a "no-no"—they've made their happiness conditional. In other words, they've made their happiness dependent on the presence of a particular set of circumstances. As long as the circumstances exist, they're happy. But when those circumstances are gone, so is the happiness.

While working, our lives had been on autopilot for many years. We didn't realize we were dependent on work or other external circumstances for happiness. And that dependence was based on feelings we derived from the circumstances.

Don't berate yourself for making your happiness conditional. There are few people who don't depend on their circumstances for happiness. But if we already feel good about ourselves, we shouldn't need the feelings we got from work (or from any other situation) to make us happy.

## *The Realities of Life and Death*

I've had many patients who suffered major losses but still appeared content. The ideal spot to get to is to feel happy just being alive. If you can get to that point, you'll be extremely grateful for all the gifts in your life.

In nature, there is no retirement. Animals compete for food and other resources right up until their deaths. We humans are blessed with retirement, a time when we no longer have to compete for jobs, promotions, or accolades. Of course, we must be financially prepared and still respect the laws of nature. But if we keep our wants and needs in perspective, it's easier to enjoy life. If we're desperately hanging onto something that's gone, we're going to create suffering for ourselves and others.

Some of us don't like the idea that we are aging and have to get old. Getting older can be scary, so we want to avoid it. We see others going downhill, and we don't want that to happen to us. We also equate aging with debility and dementia. Viewing the aging process negatively can make us feel negative about life. The reason some people become melancholic during retirement is because of their perception of aging. They notice they're physically and mentally declining. Hormone levels are also on the decline, resulting in unwelcome, sometimes embarrassing, situations. Their stamina is not as good. They can't stay up as late at night or do certain physical activities as well. These changes can be traumatic.

The best way to handle the changes that come with getting older is to accept aging as a natural part of life. Working on staying healthy both mentally and physically can slow the aging process. Staying active and engaging with younger people can keep us staying young at heart. With technology, we can be in contact with younger relatives by computer. Learning and keeping up with technology advances can boost our self-esteem.

A major issue in our culture that makes aging difficult is that most of us avoid thinking and talking about death. Most of us don't have the time or the inclination to contemplate it. We think we'll live forever, or at the very least, outrun mortality for a long time. It may dawn on us that we'll die someday when our parents die or a close friend passes on. For most of us, this realization will last for only a short time before we resume our lives without paying too much heed to our eventual demise.

But when we retire, the reality of death smacks us right in the face. It can no longer be avoided. This realization can add to our disillusionment and melancholy because, ultimately, we must all accept that death is an unpredictable and inevitable reality.

I once went to the funeral of an elderly acquaintance. At the funeral home, all of his awards and medals were laid out on a table, and a large number of people were attending. Despite these signs of his success and popularity, I wondered whether he had really enjoyed his life. When the speakers talked about him in an affectionate, loving manner, my question was answered. They talked about his personality, his uniqueness, and some of the antics he had pulled. It appeared to me that he was able to accomplish a lot and still retain his individuality. He had used his distinctive talents and qualities to enjoy life and better the lives of those he had contact with. It became clear to me that he had lived a remarkable life and one most would want to emulate. Going to funerals can be enlightening and educational. They may give us ideas on what we need to change to live a more memorable life. Plus, becoming better acquainted with the reality and inevitability of death can help us deal with the fear of dying.

Developing friendships with older people can help you learn how others are dealing with the prospect of death. Becoming more aware of death prior to retirement will help you live your life with more intention. When you fully accept that your life will not last forever, you will live more deliberately and work toward positive growth. Being aware of the finality of death can work as an incentive to live your life more fully.

### Remove Resentment from Your Life

Holding resentment into retirement will definitely result in a negative experience. Resentment is caustic, so it must be eliminated. Make a list of all your resentments—all the anger-causing, guilt-inducing, and shame-provoking situations in your life—and one by one, let them go. Forgive the people involved and forgive yourself. You'll feel a lot lighter by doing so, and it will free you to have the great retirement you deserve.

Get rid of the emotional baggage you've been holding on to—anger, resentment, guilt, shame, and worry. These are big energy drains, and they can lead to mental and physical health problems. Remember that emotional baggage is directly related to your thoughts. The person we're angry with may not even be in our lives anymore, but the anger persists because we keep it in our minds in the form of thoughts. These thoughts can be changed to be more positive.

It's hard to progress and move on with your life if you're mired in the past. Resentment kills you from the inside out. It can lead to depression and physical health problems.

Having resentment and bitterness gives us a reason to remain angry, which can cause a whole array of medical and psychological problems. High blood pressure, heart disease, and immune system problems are just a few of them. We also lose our peace of mind when we have bitterness and resentment. The people you're resentful toward most likely aren't giving you any thought, so you're only harming yourself.

After working many decades, it would be a rare individual who didn't have some ill feelings toward work or fellow workers. We all have disagreements and altercations in the workplace. Maybe someone stabbed you in the back or you were overlooked for a promotion; however, harboring feelings of resentment related to these disappointments can derail your happiness and preclude positive growth. After I retired, I was getting my house ready to sell. I called a person about putting insulation in my attic. He informed me that he had retired, but he hadn't yet taken his ads off the Internet or out of the phonebook. He went on to complain about former customers and how he had been mistreated by them. He had been retired for more than two years, but he was still hanging on to a lot of negativity.

I had some resentment after I retired. I was looking for someone to blame. I felt as though I had been taken advantage of in some situations, but after reflecting on them, I changed my point of view. The people I had bitterness toward had really done me a favor. Again, we create reality through our perceptions. You can create reality through a victim mentality, or you can accept that problems are a part of life and then move on.

If you let go of resentments about the past, you'll be much happier, and the energy you were wasting in being bitter, you can use for creativity and positive growth.

### Remove Worry from Your Life

Worry can be another retirement wrecker. It accomplishes very little while consuming a great deal of time and energy. We all worry, and some people worry much more than others. Worrying may be hereditary, but I think it's mostly a learned behavior that can be unlearned.

We tend to believe that worrying will lead to a desired outcome or circumvent an unpleasant consequence, but that's not the case. If worrying prompts you to take action in some positive way, then it can be beneficial, but that's not the worry I'm referring to.

Most worry is a waste of time, and it can also lead to depression and health issues. The body responds to worry the same way it would to an actual event. If you worry that something bad is going to happen to you, the physiologic changes that occur in your body are the same as if the event was happening to you. Adrenaline surges through your body, your blood pressure increases, and your breathing changes. Worrying over a prolonged period can deplete the body's stores of energy. This depletion can result in many mental and physical health problems.

Our nervous system is designed to handle short bouts of stress, and then it recovers. It isn't designed to handle long periods of stress. A person who worries a lot is constantly running in an energy-deficient state. We have no control over most events that happen to us, so worrying rarely helps. I'm not saying we can never worry, but we have to limit the amount of time we spend doing it and the intensity of it.

What has helped me reduce my worrying is asking myself every morning whether I have anything to be concerned about on that specific day: my health and my family's health, finances, property, and belongings. If everything is okay and nothing needs to be addressed, I try to let go of those worries for another day.

Another way to reduce worrying is to allow yourself a set period of time every day to worry about issues in your life. Give yourself thirty minutes to worry about everything you're concerned about. After you're done, if there's anything you need to take action about, do so immediately. If there's nothing that requires action, you're done worrying for the day.

The tendency to worry can be addicting because most of the things we worry about don't happen. Then we tend to believe that it was the worrying that prevented the negative outcome. You can see how this can become a difficult habit to break. Most events happen randomly, so there is nothing we can do to prevent them. It's always a good idea to take precautions when necessary, but to worry over those things we have no control over is useless.

When we have more time available, we may become preoccupied with worry. Some of us will worry about health issues, real or imagined, and others may worry about finances, family, or about the possibility of having an accident. Anything can become a source of potential worry.

Once retired, I became more aware of my ability to worry. That ability hadn't been as evident when I was working, although it must have been always present. After I retired, I was more concerned and worried than I had been in the past whenever I noticed an ache or pain.

Now that I'm aware of the function of this worry, I try not to waste too much time doing it. Pay attention to what you're worrying about. Are you needlessly staying awake at night, worrying about something that most likely won't happen? Are you ruminating about the past or the future? The past is gone and the future hasn't happened yet.

We can either involve ourselves with interesting activities that will keep us from worrying, or we can start to recognize when we're worrying and work on reducing those thoughts. Most of the things we worry about will never happen, and if they do, then we'll have suffered twice, the first time with the worry and the second time with the actual event, so isn't it best to make the situation as painless as possible and skip the initial worrying?

Take control and change whatever it is you can control. Whatever you can't control and change, you can learn to accept. I remember talking to a patient about an abnormal blood test that was a strong indication that cancer might be present. I told the patient not to worry because the diagnosis wasn't absolute and more tests were needed. His reply was, "I'm not going to worry. I don't want to be dead before I die." It took over two weeks to get the results of all the tests, and during that time, he didn't lose a wink of sleep. In the end, there was no cancer, and I was in awe of this person's ability to master the art of non-worry.

A great way to raise your self-esteem is to know that whatever happens, you'll be able to handle it. Trying not to worry continues to be a work in progress for me, but I know I'm improving and will keep at it. Just be aware of worry and don't let it take over your life.

Remember, whatever we use to keep unwanted thoughts and emotions at bay can become addicting. Even worry can be addicting. If we can identify the thoughts and emotions we want to avoid, then the worry should abate. Once we are aware of our thoughts and feelings, we can begin to work on changing them. It would be a tremendous waste of time and energy if we spent most of our retirement worrying about things over which we had no control.

### Remove Guilt from Your Life

Guilt is another prescription for a lousy retirement. It stifles joy and happiness; it makes us feel anxious and depressed. In retirement, it's common to feel guilty that we're not working and being productive. We may also feel guilty that we didn't accomplish as much as we would have wished. Guilt may arise from how we treated other people or from not spending as much time as we would have liked with our children and spouses. We can feel guilty about anything and everything if we want to.

Guilt is a useless feeling that only steals your joy. Unless you can make amends or change something for the better, guilt is a complete waste of time.

Guilt is an extremely common feeling. People use it to manipulate and pressure others to get something they want. You may have used guilt in that way. But most of the time we use guilt as a way of torturing ourselves. We allow it to occupy way too much time in our lives. Most of the things we feel guilty over are just thoughts and have no real basis.

Since I've retired, I've met many people who have retired early and don't feel guilty about it at all. You may run into trouble with guilt-induced feelings when you socialize with old chums from work. They may not understand your desire to move on with your life and do something other than work. They may try to make you feel guilty, but don't fall for it. You're on a different trajectory, and they just don't understand. That's okay because you can live your life and they can live theirs. You should seek out like-minded people who enjoyed themselves while working but were able to make the move into retirement.

Guilt was a problem for me at first because I worked in a rural area where there was a shortage of medical people. But over time, I realized I had given twenty-five years of my life in practice and thirty-three years in the medical field. Those were the best years of my life, so now it was someone else's turn.

Let go of all the guilt in your life and let in the delight. It takes time, but with awareness and understanding, it can happen.

If there is someone you have wronged or some circumstance that is causing you to feel guilty, by all means rectify the situation if possible. Clear your conscience of this negative feeling to allow more room for positivity.

### Remove the Green Monster

*Merriam-Webster's Collegiate Dictionary, Eleventh Edition* defines envy as: painful or resentful awareness of an advantage enjoyed by another joined with a desire to possess the same advantage. We all can be envious at times, but most of the time, that envy is insignificant and short-lived. The problem arises when it is intense and lasts for a long time. When this situation occurs, it can prevent the feeling of wellbeing and can also lead to disease. Envy is a problem with our sense of self, and we feel threatened when someone has something we don't. We feel like we are being denied that something. It is a feeling of inadequacy and inferiority that results in unhappiness and possible depression. The feeling is difficult to describe, but we all know it is very unpleasant.

The opportunities to be envious are many, and society seems to promote envy. The only way to keep envy at bay is to create the best life you can. Try to be truly grateful for what you have, and be happy for others when they succeed or acquire something. Don't compare yourself with others because it is not fair and only causes grief. Instead, you can use envy as a tool to get you moving and taking action, but most of the time, it just causes suffering. If you can identify what another person has, that you don't, you can work on obtaining it for yourself.

As I stated earlier, retirement can cause our self-esteem to go down, and this puts us more at risk to harbor envy. Work on improving and maintaining good, healthy self-esteem, as discussed in Chapter Five. It is essential to realize that no one has a perfect life, and good and bad happen to us all. When we are envious of someone's career success, we don't know how the rest of that person's life is going and whether he or she is truly happy. Getting a good handle on our wants and needs, as discussed in Chapter Four, will help us learn that our envy is useless. We may be envious of something we don't even want or need. This is another reason it is important to know when we have enough and our personal definition of success. It is important to remember that external things add no value to us, as individuals. Acquiring more things is not going to improve our happiness because happiness comes from within. Other people or things can't give you value or happiness.

We should begin to pay attention to the times when we are envious, and look internally to determine what is missing in our own lives. Awareness of when we feel envious and then determining the cause is the key to resolution. This is where being present in the moment can help to bring it to our consciousness, and over time, we will become more adept at recognizing envy. Also journaling about the times when we are envious can help us work through this issue.

Allow other people to be successful and have things, and realize that it doesn't change our value one bit. Learn to be happy when people have successes because everyone deserves to be happy. Envy is like a cancer that destroys us from the inside; it can be a real retirement wrecker.

Being that we are human, there may be cases when we are envious of someone and we can't resolve this envy. In those, hopefully rare, situations, we should forgive ourselves, and separate ourselves from that person. That way we have less suffering and bring no grief to the other person.

Most people haven't gained insight into their emotions, so if a person is showing signs of envy toward us, it may be best to avoid him or her. The signs that this might be going on are when a person is: hypercritical, very competitive, undermining, and manipulative.

Some people intentionally incite envy in others and enjoy being envied. These people have major self-esteem issues and should also be avoided.

"A heart at peace gives life to the body, but envy rots the bones."
— *Proverbs 14:30*

### Some Positives to Replace the Negatives

Try to become more compassionate toward people. We are all in the same boat with similar concerns and problems.

Being compassionate with ourselves and others helps to boost our self-esteem. Knowing that we're imperfect so we are going to make mistakes can make us have compassion for ourselves. We're only human, but if we learn from our mistakes, they have served a purpose. Start forgiving others and yourself; doing so can release a lot of baggage.

The world would be a better place if we all became more compassionate. Our society rewards competition and striving to get ahead at all costs. The behaviors that may have served you well while working can sometimes cause problems in retirement. Hopefully, we eventually realize we're all in the same boat. All of us are just trying to live the best lives we can; we don't have to put others down or compete with them to get ahead in life. Try to view others with more compassion and understanding. This will ultimately lead to improved happiness.

And start being more compassionate with yourself. You're just an imperfect human just like everyone else. We're all products of our upbringing and personal experiences. None of us share exactly the same experiences, so we may not totally understand other people's behaviors and views. Even siblings growing up in the same household can be vastly different in their behaviors and viewpoints. If you will be more compassionate with yourself, you will be more capable of giving compassion to others. People may act or live in a way that's counter to what you believe to be "normal," but that doesn't mean you're right. You have no idea what kind of life they've had or what's going on in their minds.

Try not to preach to people about your views or values; you'll only alienate them and frustrate yourself. Give advice only when asked, and don't be disrespectful when doing so. Some people have endured tremendous hardship and are just doing the best they can.

When I was practicing medicine, I would ask people about their lives and what rough situations they had encountered. Some of their stories were overwhelming and extremely humbling. Their tragedies were astounding in many cases.

Never judge a book by its cover; the same goes for people. When you're compassionate, you're looking at the big picture and not just through your own limited view. Just because you may have been able to navigate better in certain areas of your life doesn't mean you're superior in all aspects of life. No one is going to share your exact aspirations, dreams, goals, and values. Accept that everyone is different, and be understanding and welcoming of this fact.

We all know prejudiced people. Do they seem happy? You don't have to agree with everyone, and you don't have to be everyone's friend, but you can accept other people's differences. Try to remember when someone was compassionate toward you. You can give those good feelings back to others by being compassionate. Some people are naturally more empathetic than others, but even if you're empathetically challenged, you can still develop it.

Remember, empathy is not sympathy. Empathy is putting yourself emotionally in another person's shoes by attempting to understand what that person is going through. Sympathy is when you feel sorry for someone. Most people don't want pity; they want understanding. Sharing similar experiences with people and developing empathy for them will help you relate better to others and build stronger, longer-lasting relationships. We all need people and relationships in our lives. All of us want to be listened to and understood. Respecting people's differences and taking a sincere interest in what's going on in their lives can build bonds with people you may need during your retirement years. These skills will also improve your chances of making and keeping new friends.

It seems as though our society is becoming less and less empathetic, and this change appears to be affecting all areas of society. The ability to empathize with people is a great asset and should be given freely. Giving empathy to others is a wonderful way to help humanity and it sets a great example for our youth. In a world that seems to feel that showing empathy is weak, we, as individuals, can work to prove those feelings wrong. Without the ability to empathize, humans are capable of some horrific things. The future of the human race would be at risk if empathy didn't exist. As retirees, we have the time to work to reverse this trend by modeling empathy with all those we meet.

## Take Nothing for Granted

Try not to take anything for granted. Living in the Upper Peninsula of Michigan, I've come to realize that I have to get out and do things when the weather is good because it can change in an instant and I'll miss my chance. The same applies to life. If you have the ability and desire to do something now, just do it. You may never get another chance.

Nor should you take your family for granted. Our kids grow up very fast; if we take them for granted and don't try to spend time with them, we can never go back and reclaim that time. There is no guarantee, but if you invest time in your children, they most likely will want you to be involved in their lives later on. Remember that your kids didn't ask to be born, and they need love and understanding. It's our responsibility to teach them and give them the guidance that will help them become good citizens. We also must be committed to making sure they're prepared to live independently someday.

Sometimes our children don't turn out great despite having a good upbringing, but the odds are better when they have loving and understanding parents. If your kids can support themselves and are happy members of society, the burden will be off of you in retirement. You have done your job well. Respect your children's individualism and independence and encourage their development as separate people. We don't want clones of ourselves. Not allowing them to be themselves is a detriment to them, you, and society. Teaching them to be independent will most likely give them the best chance for success. By comparison, having an adult child return home to live with you can put extra strain on your retirement.

Don't take your spouse for granted. Spend some time working on your relationship. We never know when things might change. I once had a patient in his mid-fifties who was a teacher; he was offered a buyout package to retire, but he refused it because his family members were concerned about not having enough money to support their higher-end lifestyle. He really wanted to retire but followed along with what the family desired. Within two years of the offer, he developed a very aggressive form of cancer. At the time I left practice, he was hoping to live long enough for his daughter's wedding that was three months away.

I had a colleague in his early sixties who told me he would retire when he had a certain amount of money saved. At that time, he already had plenty of money to live comfortably. Within one year of our conversation, he developed cancer of the pancreas and died.

I could go on and on with similar true stories from my practice. I commonly saw these kinds of scenarios, and yet it still didn't dawn on me that the same thing could happen to me someday. Although I was a physician surrounded by issues of mortality, I didn't fully accept my own mortality. Don't take anything for granted.

### *Learn to Accept Change*

I have already mentioned the need to accept change, but I want to expand on that topic here. Change is difficult, and sometimes, it can be especially hard for us to accept. Change is also inevitable because without it, we could not survive. Life would be mundane without change. Therefore, it's wise to become more flexible and resilient with respect to change.

When I was a practicing physician, my work life didn't seem to change much, but everything else was changing at the speed of light. My work day was routine and structured; I ran into the same people daily and went to the same places. When I would finally slow down and spend time with family and friends, I could see all the changes occurring. The bushes and trees in our yard were getting bigger, my daughter was growing taller and advancing in school, and my wife was becoming grayer and more beautiful. My parents appeared older, friends had gotten divorced, and the list goes on and on. We get so caught up in a small slice of our lives that we're not aware of how ephemeral the other parts are.

I appreciate that most people can't take the time to get involved with all the fringe aspects of their lives. But it's good to be aware that things change fast, and what may be here today is gone tomorrow. So, don't hesitate to do the things that are important to you, and to get involved in the areas of your life that you most enjoy. Change can cause stress, but if we're expecting it and prepared for it, we're more likely to be able to cope.

### Accept and Learn from Failure

Like everyone else, you've made mistakes in the past and are going to continue to make mistakes, but they don't have to derail you. You can learn from them and go on. The only person you can really rely on 100 percent is yourself, so it's good to form a strong and lasting relationship with yourself. If you love and care about yourself, you're more likely to take better care of yourself both mentally and physically, and as a result, you'll be better able to weather any unavoidable failures.

We all fear failure to a certain degree—some to a small extent and others to an almost paralyzing level. Most people are somewhere in between. Fear of failure has some benefits because it keeps us from attempting the impossible; at the same time, it also can put major restrictions on our lives. Everything we do has some inherent risk. Even taking no risk has a risk. Just being alive is risky.

I think fear of taking risks is genetic, and long ago, it had its survival benefits, but life is different now than it was for our ancient ancestors. Most of the risks we take will not have fatal consequences.

I have a significant fear of failure, but I've come to realize how limiting this fear can be and have worked hard at reducing it. Fear of failure can limit our opportunities and make our lives very narrow. You'll be less apt to start new activities and relationships during retirement if you're afraid of failure. We all fail at something, but we can make it into a learning experience so we can do better the next time.

Getting over our fear of failure takes effort and time. We can start by experiencing small and relatively insignificant failures and learning from them. It can be freeing to know that our lives don't change much even when we do fail. Sometimes failure results from quitting or giving up when success is within our reach, and other times, what appears to be a sure failure turns out to be a blessing. We all know of people who were fired, but who then landed a much better and more enjoyable job later on. Try to keep things in perspective, and view what you perceive to be failure as an opportunity in disguise.

### *Be Yourself as Much as Possible*

There is little chance for happiness and peace of mind when you're living an inauthentic life. The further you are from authenticity, the less happy you'll be. Authenticity is based on having control of your life; when you're *not* in control, you have to wear a lot of false masks, which is not only stressful but exhausting. When you don't make the time for reflection and contemplation, you aren't in touch with who you really are and what you want. You're living life on someone else's terms. We are all different. No two people are the same, so we don't want to live on someone else's terms.

When we were working, we had to compete with others for jobs, status, money, mates, and many other things. We competed because we all wanted the same things that seemed to be in limited supply. When we retire, we no longer have to compete, nor should we want to because our talents, desires, and goals are completely different from everyone else's. You are not competing with anyone once you retire, and if you are, you aren't living authentically. It is, of course, okay to compete in games for fun, but if you're still competing for money, status, or recognition, your retirement will be less than fruitful.

### *Develop a Contemplative Side to Your Life*

Consider developing a contemplative side to your life. Spend time in introspection and contemplation to figure out what's the best life for you. Take a sincere interest in the elderly to offer care and learn from their wisdom. Tapping into the knowledge and wisdom of the elderly is a great way to learn about ourselves and how we can improve our own lives; plus, it is usually free. It's very difficult or impossible to change our basic personalities, but we can start to work on getting to know ourselves better.

Another good thing is to set aside time during your day just to be with your thoughts. Thirty minutes would do. Find a place where you can sit comfortably and not do anything. Just sit quietly and let your thoughts come and go.

Some people can't sit for more than a few minutes without getting antsy. It takes discipline to do this activity, but it can put you in a different frame of mind. We sometimes become compulsive about having to be busy all the time. This exercise starts to break you of that habit, and hopefully, you will get to the point where you will look forward to it every day.

If you can't sit for thirty minutes by yourself without anything to do, work on it gradually. Start with just a few minutes of sitting, and slowly increase the time you spend doing it. If you have to, force yourself to sit. You're trying to break the habit of always having to be entertained. If you're always giving into your compulsions, they will control you. You may actually be addicted to activity and entertainment. If you can't sit by yourself quietly for thirty minutes, you don't enjoy your own company. This could indicate a self-esteem issue. Work on it.

When you do sit in contemplation, be grateful for all the good that has happened to you and that you have in your life. Sometimes we overlook all the things that are going well and just concentrate on what has not. What we are lacking gets all the attention. Start to be more cognizant of what is going right in your life. Don't wait until it is gone to appreciate it. Use the time in contemplation to reflect on and appreciate all your blessings.

### Write a Mission Statement

Corporations write mission statements to inform workers and clients about their business' purpose. A mission statement also helps the employees stay focused on what's most important. I would encourage you to write a mission statement that describes what you think is most important to you for how you want to live your life. As an example, here is my mission statement:

> To live a happy, honest, and benevolent life without feeling inferior, critical, judgmental, angry, resentful, greedy, or prideful. To embrace life's many wonderful experiences in a calm and relaxed way, without pressure or tension. To love and accept myself at all times and to live authentically. To enjoy the process, not just the destination.

Consider writing your own mission statement. It will help you focus on what you most want to accomplish during retirement. And you can change your mission statement as your views of retirement change. Knowing you are adhering to what is most important to you will also help reduce negativity.

## *Enjoy All Stages of Your Life*

Don't forget to enjoy the process. I cannot overemphasize this. If you're waiting to enjoy your life after you retire, you're wasting your time now. What happens if your retirement doesn't turn out like you thought it would? Then you've just passed up years of potential enjoyment waiting for retirement, with no good feelings about those years. If you can look back and say, "I made the most of all the stages of my life," then you've accomplished the ultimate reason for living.

Every part of your life should be enjoyed, even the trials. To enjoy your life, you have to be present to what's going on. If your life is on autopilot, you're passively going through life.

In a few years, some of the things you're working hard for will be insignificant. The awards and recognition will be less important. If you can look back and feel, despite the ups and downs, that your life was enjoyable, you've lived to the max. Unfortunately, we often don't realize the importance of enjoying the journey until late in life. If you haven't given that much thought to whether you are enjoying the journey, start now. If you aren't enjoying it, try to determine how you can improve it. Happiness is only in the moment. Don't let it slip by any longer.

This chapter's recommendations should help you remove negativity from your life, which should help you feel better about yourself and make room for more positivity. When you're feeling good about yourself and accepting yourself, you're more likely to live authentically. Then you'll care less about what others think of you and your actions. You'll have more confidence in trying new things, and you will be a happier person. You'll be more apt to live in the present moment because you won't be wasting time and energy worrying about the past or being self-critical. Being who you really are and living as much as possible in the present moment are the keys to happiness and peace of mind. Take responsibility for claiming the life you want and living it to the fullest. Remember, following the being RETIRED philosophy, raising your self-esteem, putting a positive spin on situations, and ridding your life of negativity lead to positive growth. Positive growth eliminates PMS, making room for more positive growth, and the cycle continues. With this cycle going, your attitude is climbing at warp speed.

## Questions for Reflection

1) Are you holding any resentment that can be eliminated?

2) Do you torture yourself with guilt?

3) Would you consider yourself a worrywart?

4) Are there toxic people in your life?

5) Has envy become a problem for you?

6) Are you overlooking the good in your life and concentrating on the bad?

If you answered yes to any of the above questions, start thinking about how you can improve. Take the time to write a mission statement; it will set down in writing what is most important to you.

## Chapter Eight
## Don't Neglect Your Physical Health

WE'VE TALKED A lot about your emotional health, but your physical health is also extremely important to a satisfying retirement. Being in the best possible health will allow you to do the activities you enjoy. Your health doesn't have to be perfect, but the better shape you're in, the more options you'll have to enjoy yourself.

If you're feeling sad, tired, and depressed, it would be a good idea to see your personal physician or practitioner for a thorough exam and lab work. Sometimes an underlying health condition can be the source of melancholy. Hormone problems, vitamin deficiencies, and an assortment of other ailments can mimic PMS. Once you've ruled out a serious medical problem, you can work on improving your physical health.

According to the National Institute of Health, over two-thirds of adults are considered overweight or obese. Greater than one third of adults are obese. Nearly 75 percent of adult men are overweight. These are staggering statistics, and the numbers continue to get worse. We all know that being overweight can lead to a multitude of other problems, including diabetes, hypertension, and heart and joint problems. Our bodies work best at our ideal weight. When we go beyond this ideal weight, the organs don't work as efficiently. Fat can actually accumulate in the organs, such as the liver and heart, making it harder for them to function properly. Being overweight puts a person at higher risk for blood clots, strokes, and surgical complications.

Of course, I realize it can be very difficult to lose weight and then keep it off. There is no magic diet or exercise plan that makes losing weight any easier. Despite what the magazine articles and TV shows tell you, there really is nothing that your hard-earned money can buy that makes the weight-loss process effortless. If that were the case, those who could afford the expensive diets would be as thin as rails. We all can see that this is not the case. It all boils down to taking in less energy, in the form of food, than we burn, with activity. Under ideal circumstances, we would burn as much energy as we take in and not gain or lose. If you want to lose weight, you either have to reduce energy intake, become more active, or both. It is conceivable that a person could lose weight on a candy bar and beer diet, if energy intake is less than the energy used. That diet would not support you nutritionally, so I'm not recommending it, but I hope you get my point.

If you've become overweight, now is the time to start changing that. Getting down to your ideal body weight is the ultimate goal, but even losing 10-15 percent of your excess body weight can be beneficial. Exercising at least one hour a day can help you get in condition and bring the weight down. Getting into the habit of not eating anything between meals will also help.

Stay away from the sugar-containing soda beverages; they contain a high amount of energy. It would take you thirty minutes of brisk walking to burn off the energy, in the form of sugar, in one can of soda. If you didn't burn it off, it would be stored as fat. If you consume one can of soda daily, and don't burn off the energy, you will gain one-and-a-third pounds every month. That is potentially fifteen pounds per year. It doesn't take much to get overweight—just one can per day—and most people drink much more. There are 3,500 calories (measure of energy) in a pound of fat and 150 calories in a can of soda. Multiply 150 calories by thirty days and you get 4,500 calories. Then divide that number by 3,500 and you get 1.28 pounds gained per month. Multiply that by twelve months and you gain over 15 pounds every year.

Any high sugar or high fructose drinks will do the same thing. One can of beer or one medium glass of wine contains approximately the same number of calories as a can of soda. Remember that one, innocuous-appearing beverage a day can cause unwanted pounds. It probably takes ten minutes to drink a soda, and all you have to do is swallow. In order to burn that energy off, you would have to walk briskly for thirty minutes. If you wait until the end of the month to work on burning off the accumulated calories, it would take fifteen hours of brisk walking. Waiting until the end of the year, it would take you 180 hours of brisk walking to burn off the extra calories. If your brisk walk is three miles per hour, you would have to walk 540 miles to burn it off. That is more than the length of half the state of California.

The calories will be burned off only if you also give up the soda. If you added some pretzels or chips to that soda, you would have to walk the rest of the way through California and into Mexico. Some drinks like specialty coffees contain a lot more calories than sodas, so avoid them if you are trying to lose weight. Dairy products are also high in calories, so it is a good idea to start cutting back on them also.

As you can see, it is a whole lot easier to gain weight than lose it. This is why you have to: 1) take inventory on what you take in, 2) cut back on how much you eat, and 3) exercise. These three steps are the only effective way to lose weight and keep it off.

In some cases, people gain weight from overeating due to emotional issues. If this is the case, then it is much harder to lose the weight and keep it off, so some form of professional assistance may be necessary.

I am not implying that it is easy to lose weight at all, but I know that by being overweight, we are at greater risk of further health problems. It may be more difficult to enjoy your retirement and life if you are suffering from the maladies associated with being overweight. I used to tell my patients that a gallon of milk weighs eight pounds so if you're twenty-five pounds overweight, you have the equivalent of three gallons of milk strapped to your waist. Just lifting a gallon of milk out of the grocery cart is hard enough, so think how carrying three of them limits your body.

If you have a weight problem, don't berate yourself; just continue to be aware of your eating habits and work to bring the weight down. We all know it is much easier to gain weight than to lose it.

Developing good sleeping habits is also important for maintaining good health. When in a sleep-deprived state, a whole range of potential problems can occur. Insomnia can happen as a result of both medical and psychological problems. The causes of insomnia are varied and beyond the scope of this book, but if you are suffering from insomnia, it is important to find the cause and correct it. Lack of sleep can result in memory problems, concentration difficulties, and even depression. Prolonged sleep deprivation can lead to hypertension, heart disease, and strokes. Our immune systems can also be negatively affected, making us more susceptible to viral and bacterial infections. Weight gain has also been associated with long-term sleep problems. The symptoms of sleep deprivation can also mimic those of dementia, like Alzheimer's. Most people require 7-9 hours of sleep a night. Some can get by on less, but the majority of us require at least seven.

Most sleep problems will respond to adopting what is referred to as a sleep hygiene, if they are not the result of a medical condition. Sleep hygiene means preparing yourself for sleep with a ritual and eliminating distractions. Try to make sure your bedroom is free from distractions like a TV or computer. If you can avoid working on anything that takes a lot of concentration an hour before bedtime, do so. Get in the routine of going to bed at the same time every night. If you are having trouble sleeping during the night, do not take a nap during the day to catch up. Don't ingest any caffeine after 12 p.m. Try to get physical exercise every day.

Sometimes emotional problems and even PMS can result in insomnia. Once the cause of the emotional problem is identified and resolved, the insomnia will improve. It is not unusual to have an occasional fitful night's sleep; you most likely will catch up the next night. An afternoon nap can be refreshing, but only take one if it won't upset your nighttime sleep. Avoid taking any sleep aids for more than a night or two because they can be habit forming.

Be aware that over the counter medicines can be dangerous if used improperly. A lot of medications, sold over the counter, are the same or chemically related to prescription medications, just at a lower dosage. These medications may have untoward side effects that are not readily known. I can't tell you how many times I saw patients who had major complications due to benign-appearing medications they had purchased without a prescription; some patients nearly destroyed their livers and kidneys, and others had severe intestinal bleeding as a result.

Many of these medications contain stimulants that can cause insomnia and raise your blood pressure. They can also interact with some of the medications you are already on, resulting in unwanted and possibly dangerous side effects. You could also develop a serious allergy to these meds. As we age, the functioning of our organs declines, so the recommended dosages may not be appropriate but too high and need to be adjusted. Use these drugs with caution and discuss the appropriateness of usage with your practitioner. Many hospitalizations and office visits are due to complications with medications.

If you smoke, now is the time to quit. Smoking is one of the worst habits we can have. Numerous health problems are directly linked to cigarette smoke. Increased lung infections, arterial problems, heart disease, emphysema, and lung cancer are just a fraction of the illnesses that can occur as the result of smoking. Smoking complications are related to how long a person has smoked and the number of cigarettes smoked per day. In the course of a lifetime, a person smoking one pack per day can smoke over 200,000 cigarettes. Unfortunately, some people smoke much more than this.

As we age, our lung capacity declines, so if you smoke, the effect on breathing is increased. Smoking is a difficult habit to break because the nicotine in tobacco is highly addictive. I know it is possible to quit because I have witnessed it numerous times with patients in my practice. The majority, however, quit after they developed a tobacco-related illness.

Having a dependence on tobacco can potentially damage your retirement. You could be facing a hacking cough, emphysema, chronic obstructive pulmonary disease, more frequent pneumonia, and a higher risk of lung cancer. All of these problems can reduce the quality of your life. Having to wear an oxygen mask and carry an oxygen tank wherever you go can be very limiting. Only being able to walk very short distances, because of lung disease from smoking, will eliminate the possibility of some enjoyable activities during your retirement.

Even if you have smoked for many years, some of the damage to your lungs may be reversed by quitting. Do whatever it takes to quit. There are many programs available to assist you.

If you drink alcohol, quit or at least cut way down. Alcohol is a depressant, so if you're already sad or depressed, it will only exacerbate the problem. Using alcohol as a coping mechanism is unhealthy and will only lead to more problems. Alcohol is a poison to the body. The only reason we can get away with drinking it is because the amount we take in is usually less than the amount it would take to kill us. The alcohol we ingest can negatively affect our organs. It can inflame the liver and pancreas, and it can cause the heart to beat irregularly. Our brains can be affected; in fact, prolonged drinking can lead to a form of dementia.

An occasional alcoholic beverage is fine, but drinking frequently for months to years can cause you numerous problems; even if you don't develop a health issue from the alcohol, other issues can result such as relationship and legal problems. Practice good habits: Don't drink and drive. Even small amounts of alcohol in your system can decrease your reflexes. I had a patient who had an alcoholic beverage with a meal at a restaurant. Driving home, she was involved in an accident where another person was seriously injured. Even though her alcohol level was well below the legal limit, she is still haunted by thoughts that the alcohol could have affected her driving ability.

Most of the elderly are taking medications that can possibly interact with alcohol in an adverse way. As we age, our livers don't metabolize alcohol as efficiently, and even smaller amounts can take a toll on the body. I know that excessive alcohol consumption is common in the elderly because I saw it in my practice. I had patients in the hospital, whom no one knew were drinkers, go through terrible alcohol withdrawals. Believe me, that is not a pretty sight. It is very difficult to enjoy your retirement if you have an alcohol problem. Be honest with yourself and seek help if needed to reduce your alcohol consumption or quit.

The use of any drugs or alcohol for recreational purposes is potentially dangerous and should not be taken lightly.

Eliminate any other addictions. Some doctors and psychologists believe we all have problems with some form of addiction, whether it be a substance or behavior. I wouldn't go so far as to say everyone has some form of addiction, but addictions are common. Addictions can develop for many reasons. Our culture and lifestyles seem to promote addictive behaviors. Society even glorifies certain addictions like overworking or being materialistic and buying too many things we don't need. Some genetic predisposing factors may also make people more prone to addictions, but most addictions result from stress, how we feel about ourselves, and our looking for a way to cope with life's difficulties.

Don't wait until you retire to deal with your addiction; start as soon as possible. It is best to address any addictions you may have prior to retirement, but retirement can be an ideal time to delve into what may be causing your addictive behavior. Some of your problems may stem from past experiences or traumas. Now you can explore the possible reasons for the addiction and address them. Retirement can be a time when you can get to know yourself, learn to like yourself, and change unwanted behaviors. In my opinion, this is the most precious gift that retirement offers. I know I had an addiction to work. Because I have looked into the cause, I now understand the reason and how it happened. I have had the time to study it, which I didn't have prior to my retirement.

Getting rid of any addiction is going to take some work, but it is well worth the effort. An addiction is anything you would crave if you gave it up. Any addiction will make it difficult to have a good attitude because it will be competing for the time and attention required to develop a good attitude. It also can be costly, both financially and healthwise. Addictions will bring more negativity into our lives and reduce the possibility of positivity.

Addictions also control us because we have to live according to the availability of whatever we are addicted to. This is not a pleasant way to live. I remember driving to a hunting camp sixty miles away with some other hunters, during an ice storm. We came across numerous cars in the ditch during that white-knuckle ride. What would have normally taken an hour took nearly three. When we arrived at the camp, one of the other hunters realized he had forgotten his carton of cigarettes. The rest of us were secretly happy about it because of the absence of the annoying smoke and the opportunity for him to give up smoking. However, this hunter panicked, got back in the car, and drove thirty miles to a convenience store. I think most smokers could identify with this story, but I remember thinking, *What a terrible way to live.*

If you have addictions, do whatever it takes to rid yourself of them. You can do introspection, counseling, or join a Twelve-Step program. If you have severe problems with addiction, seek proper medical treatment. I don't think you can fully appreciate retirement if you are dealing with addictions. Be honest with yourself and don't give up your power to some substance or behavior—you deserve a better life.

It is also very important that you eat healthy and nutritious foods. Eating too many processed and fatty foods can lead to health problems. The grocery stores are full of snack foods, most of which have no nutritional value at all. The crunchy foods found in the bags, in most cases, are just converted to sugar and stored in the body as fat. Start reading labels and keep track of calories, sugar grams, and fat grams. Limit your intake of sugar. Fast foods should also be limited because it doesn't take much for the calories to add up, and a lot of fast foods are high in fat. I don't recommend a particular diet; just be aware of what you are ingesting and read labels. Avoid high-salt, high-fat, and high-sugar foods. Eat fruits, vegetables, nuts, and lean meats. Check with your doctor if you are supposed to be following a certain diet or eliminating some foods. If all you are eating is junk food, you will not feel well. You also will be more susceptible to medical problems like high blood pressure and high cholesterol. Use common sense when picking foods to eat. If you don't understand anything about what to eat and what not to eat to remain healthy, make an appointment with a dietician. A plethora of books are available to educate yourself, and doing a Google search of healthy foods will yield many websites to peruse. Having a well-balanced intake of foods is as good as or better than most of the popular diets.

Physical exercise is very important to good health. As I mentioned in the weight-loss section above, it is beneficial, and in most cases necessary, to lose and keep off excess weight. Exercise that involves weight-bearing can keep our bones and muscles strong. Weight-bearing exercise is where you are using your own body weight to strengthen the bones and muscles. Examples of this type of exercise are: walking, running, and jumping rope. The main reasons to do this form of exercise are that it helps to keep the muscles from atrophying and can prevent osteoporosis. It can also help us maintain good balance. Physical exercise can reduce blood pressure, lower cholesterol, and prevent diabetes. Elderly people who exercise have a reduction in mortality and improved cognitive function. Studies have shown that exercise works as well as medication for treating depression. Doing physical activity daily can improve sleep habits. I recommend an hour of physical activity each day, but as little as fifteen minutes per day has been shown to be beneficial. It doesn't have to be elaborate exercise; just a brisk walk will do. People with limitations can still exercise, in most cases, but the activity may need to be tailored based on their tolerance. If you have questions about the type of exercise you could do, talk to your doctor or a physical therapist.

Getting out into nature can greatly improve your mood. We are part of the animal kingdom, so it is best to have some exposure to our natural environment. Being inside buildings with artificial lighting and air modification day after day is not healthy; however, most of our jobs require us to be indoors all day. If, after work, we hop in the car, drive home, and then sit in front of the computer or TV all night, it's not much different to living the life of a zoo animal. The animals may be alive, but they're not living as they were born to live. I remember seeing a bear in a zoo that kept walking around in circles. He was alive, but he surely wasn't acting like a bear.

Numerous reasons exist to get outside and be with nature. The most important reason is that it is healthy and relaxing. You can put your troubles behind you and just observe what is happening around you. Watching the birds and other animals can be healing. Being by a stream or other body of water can be tranquilizing. Getting out in nature can also provide a welcome break from technology, provided you turn it off or, better yet, leave it behind. If you live in the country, it is easy to find places to go to be with nature. In the city, it may be harder, but there are parks and nature walks in most municipalities. If you have a dog, both of you could get some exercise and fun too. The fresh air and sun energizes us. We also sleep better at night after we are outdoors, and it can improve our mood. It's a good idea to incorporate some form of outdoor exercise into your schedule before you retire. With time, outdoor exercise can become an important part of your lifestyle.

Start by taking walks or gardening—anything to get outside. I know this may be different from what you've been hearing from the medical community, but sunlight is important to our health. You don't have to spend hours in direct sunlight, which can be harmful without sun protection, but just being outdoors on a sunny day can boost your spirits and increase your vitamin D levels. Vitamin

D is important for normal bone development, and low levels in the body have been linked to depression. If you live in the country, start hiking, kayaking, biking, or gardening. Observing birds and other wildlife is much better than reality TV. If you live in the city, go to parks or find walking areas close to where you live. Consider joining a nature or outdoors club. Whatever gets you outside is fine because it's important for good mental health.

As I've mentioned earlier, social interaction is necessary for a happy life. Its health benefits, both physically and mentally, are well-known. It's not good to be isolated, and it is harder to develop social outlets if you become isolated. Innumerable possibilities exist for socialization. Find groups or people with similar interests and get involved. Volunteer, go to workshops or lectures or plays, or do whatever gets you out and about. The happiest people are the ones doing things with others. You may be more of an introvert, but don't let that stop you from doing something social once or twice a week. Keeping a social network going will also be of benefit if you lose a spouse or significant other. As a doctor, I saw many elderly people who felt lost after the death of a spouse because they hadn't nurtured any relationships outside of their marriage.

### *Pay Attention to How You Handle Stress*

Stress can cause both physical and mental health issues. Our bodies and minds are not designed to endure chronic stress, so it's important to limit long-term stress as much as possible. First, be aware of how you handle stress. Are you smoking or drinking too much? Is your weight becoming a problem from overeating? If your coping strategies are less than healthy, you need to start changing them. Otherwise, the same bad habits you had before retirement will follow you into retirement and will most likely get worse because of the extra time on your hands. It's much harder to change these habits when you're experiencing the stressful stages of retirement—better to change them beforehand.

It's easy to fall into long-term survival mode when we're under a lot of stress. We may start neglecting the important things in life, like family and friends. The survival mode is a chronic state of "fight or flight." We have increased levels of adrenaline and cortisol. Adrenaline is a stimulant that prepares us to react to a threat. Cortisol is a steroid that functions as an anti-inflammatory; it is similar to the medication that doctors give for allergic reactions and joint injections. The elevation of these two chemicals for a short period of time can be beneficial because they help us deal with short-term stress, but if elevated for prolonged periods, they can do damage. High blood pressure, heart disease, diabetes, and osteoporosis are just a few of the numerous illnesses that can result from prolonged high levels of adrenaline and cortisol.

Over time, our bodies gradually get so used to these elevated levels that we don't even notice them. They become our new normal, even though they are damaging our bodies. Eventually, our behaviors and how we're functioning may reveal that we have a problem, in the form of a medical or psychological concern. Unfortunately, some people have a massive stroke or fatal heart attack before ever having any real warning that something is brewing. Some early indicators that you may have a problem with stress are insomnia, irritability, fatigue, and lack of enjoyment in life. Often, a loved one will notice a change in your behavior, such as a lack of attentiveness.

It's very important to recognize whether you're in survival mode because it's incompatible with an enjoyable life. It's also very difficult to eradicate this mode because it develops over time and is brought on by one's lifestyle. Start to pay attention to your lifestyle and behaviors, and if you're having problems with prolonged stress, begin addressing it right away (hopefully, before you retire).

The last thing you want to do is start retirement while in survival mode. Your body will be geared up for stress, but because your retirement lifestyle will be less stressed, you may go through a form of adrenaline withdrawal, or your body may try to keep you stimulated so the levels stay up. You would be, in a sense, all revved up with no place to go. Be aware that stress can be a potential problem and start to change your behavior. You can work on relaxation, spending less time wrapped up in work, and attending to your own and your family's needs. Just being aware of the stress in your life is a start. You may be creating some of your own stress, so look for areas where you can eliminate or reduce it.

When certain stresses can't be reduced or eliminated, we can work on our reactions to that stress as described previously. Finding some way to relax can be beneficial to stress reduction. Some people find meditation to be of benefit, while others like yoga. Do whatever works for you. Herbert Benson wrote a book many years ago called *The Relaxation Response*. It explains how people can turn down their stress response throughout the day. By learning some of these techniques, we are educating ourselves on how to recognize when we are stressed and how we, individually, can reduce that stress. Learning techniques to help you tolerate stress can only benefit you and improve your quality of life.

The presence of stress in our lives is normal; if you are alive and breathing, you will experience some form of stress. Try to remove the stressors you can remove and work on learning to change how you react to the stresses that are unavoidable. Remember, your reactions to stress are based on your thoughts, and your thoughts can be changed or your situation can be looked at in a new way.

### *Be Alert to Changes in How You Feel*

We all have been wounded in some way. Childhood traumas, relationship problems, and life's stresses can affect us profoundly.

It's wise to be alert to changes in the way you feel and to any mental or physical problems that can't be explained. Such issues may indicate that your life is out of sync, so your mind or body are trying to tell you something is wrong. If you have no organic issues that can account for your physical symptoms, that's a warning that some life problem exists and will only get worse if not addressed. It may indicate that some form of change in your life is needed, and if the problem goes on for too long, it can lead to permanent consequences.

When you're having psychological symptoms related to your life situation, the cause of these symptoms can go unrecognized and result in life-changing mental and physical health issues. Again, it's so important to ask yourself why these things might be occurring; then, you may be able to identify sources of stress in your life and work on eliminating them.

More than 70 percent of visits to the family doctor are because of stress-related problems. I saw this in my own practice, and I'm sure the rashes I used to get were due to stress. I was amazed by how many of the patient visits I saw were stress-related. Some people willingly accepted and, in fact, were relieved to hear that their illnesses were stress-related and psychologically-based. Others could not believe they had a stress-related problem, so they continued to go from doctor to doctor looking for a physical cause. You'll be less likely to enjoy your retirement if your health fails you. There are many well-known physicians and other respected professionals who feel that the mind plays a part in every disease. I am not sure that all diseases are brought on by our mental states, but I know it has a role in the clear majority. Just try to be aware of the changes and stressors occurring in your life and how they are linked to the mind. Your health and how you feel will be affected by them. It is possible that by addressing the stress in your life, your health or any unhealthy symptoms will improve. If you stay attuned to your body, you may be able to prevent a major problem. This is where loving who you are and caring about yourself is so important. If you care about yourself, you're more likely to take interest in maintaining your physical and mental health.

With that in mind, it is important that you find a primary care physician, nurse practitioner, or physician assistant who listens and asks questions about what is happening in your life. It is only through this interest that the proper diagnosis and treatment plan can be derived. It is also imperative that you be willing to share this information with the practitioner. It is nearly impossible to get an accurate assessment with only half of the available data. To stay healthy, you need to take an active role in your medical care. Medical personnel can only help you if you are honest and open. Be aware that these same medical people are not perfect and that they will not always be right. If you are uncomfortable with a diagnosis, treatment, or planned procedure, seek a second opinion. Even though practitioners have similar training and take the same exams, their experiences are not the same. A practitioner who wants the best for you will be receptive to your request for other input. If your practitioner becomes defensive or insulting, it is time to go shopping.

Know your family medical history and share it with your practitioner. With this knowledge, you can work on staving off or preventing a disease that you are genetically predisposed to develop. My father developed diabetes in his forties, so I have taken measures, like weight management and exercise, in the hopes I can keep it at bay. So far so good. This is your life and your health is very important, so guard it closely.

Discuss with your practitioner the need for cancer screening. Some of the worst forms of cancer can be screened for and detected at a stage where treatments are most effective. You may be at greater risk for certain cancers, based on your lifestyle and genetics, so it may be wise to have screenings before and more often than what is commonly recommended. Don't forget to keep up with your vaccinations because they are one of the easiest ways to prevent disease. Try to record when your vaccinations were done so that if you move or are seen in an emergency room, you can inform the appropriate people.

Accidents can happen quickly and unexpectedly, but many are due to not paying attention to what we are doing. We must try to stay mindful during activities. I saw a lot of patients who had broken bones and severe lacerations because of not having their full attention on an activity. Pay attention to your footing when ascending or descending stairs and when walking on irregular or slippery terrain. Take the recommended safety precautions when using potentially dangerous equipment. Use protective eye- and ear-ware when necessary. I had a patient lose an eye fixing a garage door opener without a protective lens. I broke my right index finger while walking and trying to read the paper at the same time. Things can happen fast even when you take the care to be cognizant of what you are doing, but you may be able to reduce the likelihood or seriousness of an accident by instituting safety measures.

Remember that following the being RETIRED philosophy, having high self-esteem, putting a positive spin on things, getting rid of negativity, and optimizing your health lead to positive growth. Positive growth relieves PMS, which can lead to further positive growth, and the cycle continues. By following the above recommendations, your attitude will rise at warp speed.

### Questions for Reflection

1) How would you rate your health? Why?

2) How can you get more exercise?

3) How is your diet?

4) Do you have stresses that can be reduced?

5) What diseases are found in your family?

6) Do you have any bad habits that can adversely affect your health?

Chapter Nine
# Plan for Lifelong Financial Health

BEFORE WE GET into the ways we can become and remain financially independent, I would like to digress a little. Over the years,
I have had a great interest in people and their personalities. I have
studied different personality types and the disorders associated with
them.

We sometimes say that we love or hate our jobs, as if our job were a
real person, and we take it personally if we are let go or fired from the
job. For fun, let's pretend our job is an actual person with a personality
of its own. So what personality type is your job? I think the personality
type that best fits a job is the narcissistic personality. A person with
a narcissistic personality actually has a disorder in which the ability
to show empathy is absent. True emotions are also not shown, and as
long as things go the narcissist's way, everything will appear to be fine.
Narcissistic personalities can come across as being kind, but will be
manipulative in many ways. This is a very simplified description of a
very complex disorder, but understand that you will get no emotional connection from a person with a narcissistic personality. I am not
a psychotherapist or psychiatrist, but I think the following ideas will
stick better if given as a human interaction. So here goes.

If you are unaware that you are in a relationship with a narcissist,
you are under great risk of being used and abused. The narcissist will
give you no love in return and will use you for his or her benefit. Narcissists want you to become dependent on them so they can control
you. Once you start having problems with narcissists or you try to buck
them, they either punish or get rid of you. When you are doing what

they want, they will treat you okay and may even give you rewards, but the terms change when you challenge them.

A job is similar to a narcissist because you will get no love or empathy from it, and you will get rewarded only in cold hard cash. When you can no longer comply with the work demands, for whatever reason, you are reprimanded or let go. At times, you can be discarded in an inhumane fashion, for no obvious cause. While I was working, I once saw a worker of thirty years escorted out of the building by security after being let go—as if he were a criminal. I saw employees lose their pensions, benefits, and dignity after being fired. A job can be as heartless as a narcissistic partner.

So, what do you do if you discover yourself in a narcissistic relationship? First and foremost, you separate yourself emotionally and financially from the narcissist and gain independence. You need to become the master of your own destiny and be able to survive without the narcissist. The previous chapters of this book helped you separate emotionally from your job. Now we will look into how you can get and stay financially separate from it.

As I've stated before, our jobs can provide many benefits, but it is best to have the ability to exist when the job ends. I don't want you to get the impression that your job is your enemy, but I hope this example will leave a lasting imprint. Your job will never love you back, and at times, it can be disappointing and life-disrupting. I can remember several years ago when the automobile companies were making major cuts in employment and the newspapers were full of articles in which people were commiserating and venting. Some people's lives were drastically changed, and most were unprepared for this situation. I also remember one article, during the same period, in which a seasoned worker was talking about being laid off. She had lived through massive layoffs before, so she had saved money in the event that it happened again. She stated that she was going to use the layoff to spend more time with family and do the things she'd had no time for previously. She was looking forward to the time off, and it wasn't going to upset her current lifestyle at all. Enough of the digression; let's get started.

It's hard to enjoy your retirement if you're constantly worried about money. Your fiscal health is as important as your physical health; in some cases, it's more important. If you're in very poor physical health, you're going to need the money to pay for the care, and the expenses associated with illness can really add up. Your income now will be coming from investments, a pension (if you're lucky enough to have one), and Social Security.

What has taken me by surprise during retirement is the unexpected money demands—home maintenance, car maintenance and repair, dental emergencies, and taxes on investments. All of these can be unpredictable and pricey. It's very important to prepare financially for retirement rather than have to rely on the government for support.

Some of the practices brought out in this book will not be appropriate for you, but others may be worth considering. Some may appear unconventional, unorthodox, annoying, and even anti-American. But what could be more American than living financially free in a free society?

Let's get the disclaimer out of the way first. These suggested examples will not make you rich, but they may help you become and/or stay financially independent. Some have been written tongue-in-cheek, but my hope is that you become more attuned to the many ways of saving money. Most of the examples I have put into practice myself, or I have learned an important lesson from not doing so.

I know what you are thinking, *It's easy to save money when you are making a lot of money.* I know this because I would be thinking the same thing—that being a doctor, lawyer, or some other professional really gives you an advantage. To some extent, that may be true, but remember, most professions demand extra time in school and entail additional costs associated with that education. Most doctors don't start making any real money until they are in their thirties. During their education years, they are not able to save any money. They are not paying much into Social Security, and they finish their training with a heap of debt. A person who starts saving and investing earlier has a significant lead, so it can take the professional many years to catch up.

Start looking at the life you have and what you can change to make your life less expensive and save more. Many areas in your life might be downsized to be less of a financial burden. Do you need the two cars or the travel trailer? Are you getting the use out of the time share? Begin to think about some of the areas where your money is being spent but not giving you any value. Are you paying for services that aren't being provided, or for something you can do for yourself? Start questioning where the money is going. There are also things you should consider if you are still working. If you own a business, you might think about selling it before you retire and working for the new owners for a while. No one will want to buy your business, at a good price, if it is starting to decline. Another thing to consider is dissolving any business partnerships prior to retirement. If the partnership will no longer be beneficial to you after retirement, why not end it before you retire? This includes real estate or shared properties. Having to deal with old business relationships may add to the stress you'll already be encountering in retirement.

If possible, it's a good idea to be debt-free at the time of retirement. It will give you more freedom to deal with life's issues. Having major payments hanging over your head can be a dark cloud for your retirement. If you can make the big purchases before retirement, such as a car, a new roof, or a new furnace, it will remove the need for coming up with a lot of cash all at once or eliminate having to go in debt when you're not working. Having to borrow money or sell income-producing assets to pay for a big repair or replacement can upset your cash flow.

Less than 10 percent of people will be able to support themselves in retirement. The majority will be dependent on the government or relatives for financial support. It doesn't have to be that way. Most of us were never taught how to save and invest. The way we handle money is usually a result of what we learned from parents and teachers. Some of their advice was good, but a lot was not so good. In retirement, it will be very hard to acquire more or build on your already accumulated assets because you are no longer getting an income from work. I believe most people would be better off financially if they knew how to save and invest long before they stopped working. One of the biggest regrets of retired people is that they wished they would have started saving earlier and saved more. Begin by being more conscious of your spending. Ask yourself these questions: "Do I really need this item? How much money would I recoup at a garage sale? Is this item eatable should I run out of money?"

Below, I offer suggestions that can help with this process. As I stated above, there is no guarantee that these suggestions will make you wealthy, but they can help get you in better financial shape for retirement. There are many financial books available to help you with investing.

## TOP FINANCIAL RETIREMENT TIPS

**Save at least 10 percent of your income** beyond any retirement plan provided by your employer or retirement fund. This money could be invested in index funds, with the intent that it will not be touched unless an absolute emergency occurs. It should be allowed to grow for years, and because you are adding 10 percent yearly to it, it has the opportunity to become quite large. As your income increases, so will the amount being saved. If you can afford to save more, by all means, do so. The more the better. Ten percent is the minimum, and there is no maximum.

**Only buy the house you need.** When people start making money, they look for the biggest house they can afford, not necessarily the smaller, less expensive house that will be fine for their needs. The kids grow up fast and leave home eventually, and then you are left with more house than you need. If you're working to pay for the home, you aren't enjoying it, and most of your vacations will be spent elsewhere. When you go for the bigger home, all of your expenses increase—heating, electric, insurance, maintenance, and repair expenses. Working to support a bigger home causes stress, and reselling a bigger home may be more difficult. If you already own a large home, you might consider downsizing before you retire. A larger home will have more and larger problems. When I see a big home, I just see big maintenance and big costs. The bigger the home, the bigger the responsibility. I down-sized when I retired and I haven't regretted it. My costs are way down, and the indoor and outdoor maintenance is easy to accommodate.

Another option is to rent and not bother with ownership during retirement. Look into all the different possibilities and pick the scenario that will financially be the best for you. Consider living in an area that has a lower cost of living. Sometimes living in a less-in-demand place can save you a ton of money. For example, you can get much more for your money in Michigan than you can in California. I realize you may have to go where you can find employment, but if that is not necessary, the cost difference can be astronomical if you remain in a less expensive area. The money you save on taxes and other expenses can be saved and invested for retirement, and if you then want to live somewhere else once you retire, you can afford to. Sometimes the distance doesn't have to be that great; just a few miles difference can reduce your cost of living. I lived in rural Michigan for many years, and the cost of living there was substantially less than the larger cities close by. Now I am living in a larger city, but the money I saved is earning income.

**Keep home upgrades to a minimum.** If you add upgrades, such as granite countertops and top-of-the-line cabinets, you're not likely to recoup your money when you sell. Let's say you spent $30,000 on upgrades. Once spent, that money is gone. But if you invest $30,000 at 5 percent, you would have more than $81,000 after twenty years. If you wanted to take money out monthly, that investment could pay you approximately $436.00 a month, and it would last for thirty years if you kept earning 5 percent. You would earn $5,232.00 annually from the investment. Times that by thirty years for a total of over $156,000. Depending on where the money is invested, it's possible to earn more than 5 percent. If you can afford the home upgrades you desire, by all means get them. But keeping home upgrades to a minimum is a good way to help save for retirement.

**Don't buy a second home.** For many reasons, a first home is not the best investment, so why would you want two? Second homes include camps and cottages—anything beyond your main residence. Unless you're handy and enjoy working on the upkeep, it will cost you to maintain and repair it. It will also tie up a lot of money that you may not recoup when you sell. You'll have insurance, taxes, and heating bills to pay. A second home also lessens your freedom. If you're ultra-wealthy, you can pay someone to do the maintenance. If not, it will cost you in time and cash. Instead of buying a second home, rent one. When you leave, the problems are left behind. I remember reading somewhere not to invest your retirement money in anything that requires maintenance or feeding. I think that is good advice. It can, however, increase your social life. The interactions with the plumber, painter, groundskeeper, and repair people can sometimes develop into personal friendships.

**Quit smoking.** I know we have discussed quitting smoking for health reasons, but there are other reasons to quit. Smoking can have a pernicious effect not only on your physical health but on your fiscal health as well. It can take years away from your working life and lead to increased medical expenses. The money lost to cigarettes is lost investment potential. If you and your significant other both smoke, you can double the outlay and the amount lost. If you smoke a pack a day at $6 a pack, that's $180 a month or $2,160 annually. If you invested that money at 5 percent over twenty years, it would be worth $73,986.06. If you got a monthly payment from that money over thirty years and still invested at 5 percent, it would be $397.17 or $4,766.08 annually. Once again, that cigarette money could grow for longer than twenty years and at a higher rate of return.

I realize it's not easy to quit smoking, but it's not easy to support the habit either. As mentioned before, a good reason to quit smoking is that you probably don't want to be carrying an oxygen tank wherever you go during your retirement. Smoking does have one advantage, however; it may significantly reduce your lifespan so you don't have to worry about affording your retirement.

**Get the best health insurance: your own good health.** The better your health, the less you'll have to pay in the form of deductibles and co-pays. When your health is good, you're going to be more productive. You'll lose less time from work and be more resilient in fighting off colds and other viruses. Try to exercise an hour a day. Maintain your body weight according to your body mass index (BMI) (although it's not totally accurate). Cut back on sugars, sweets, and processed foods. Purchase a blood pressure machine and check your pressure regularly. Keep your stress levels down if possible; nothing ages you faster than excessive stress. I also recommend buying and learning how to read urine dipsticks. They can help detect infections, diabetes, and certain kidney and bladder problems. If you note an abnormality in a reading, see your personal practitioner. Watch for any rashes or changes in moles on your skin, and when in doubt, have them checked out. Any changes in your bodily functions should be evaluated by a professional.

**Take good care of your teeth.** Dental problems can be painful in several ways, not only physically but to your pocketbook. Brush your teeth at least twice a day and floss prior to brushing. If you're having tooth pain, get it checked out before it gets worse. Sometimes when a tooth is infected, it can become less painful even without treatment. This can give you the false sense that everything is fine, but the pain will come back worse in the future. Dental work is expensive, but if you put off the needed attention, the expense can potentially drain your financial resources.

**Get that new car feeling without buying a new car.** Your car has some miles on it, but you want a new one. Here is what you can do to quench that expensive feeling. For three months, don't clean it. Let papers, food wrappers, dirt, and dust build up. Then spend an afternoon cleaning the car and making it spotless. You'll feel like you're in a new car, and it hasn't cost you anything more than cleaning supplies and some elbow grease.

I had a car that was already eleven years old with a lot of mileage when I hit a deer. The repairs took two weeks, so I was given a loaner by the body shop. The loaner car ran fine, but its shocks were shot and it was junky on the inside. It had tears in the seats and didn't handle very well. While my car was being fixed, I had thought about getting rid of it. But when I got it back, it felt like a luxury car compared to the loaner. I still own it, and it has been very reliable. My mechanic says, "Ride it until the wheels fall off, and when it starts to rattle, turn up the radio."

This principle can be applied to almost any possible purchase. If you think you need a new house, go camping where you live in a tent for a week or two. This might mitigate the urge to buy.

When you need to replace your car, think about buying used. Some used vehicles are in great shape and will give you years of good service for a lot less cost than a new one. Cars are a utility, not an investment, so try to buy only what you are going to need.

**Always take care of the recall problems with your car.** Not doing so can have potentially dangerous consequences and lead to more expenses down the road. Once you get the notice, it's up to you to make an appointment and take it in. I ignored a recall once and will never do it again. I had received a letter announcing a recall concerning the front wheels, and I ignored it. A few months later, the right front tire separated from the vehicle. I was fortunate to be going at a very slow speed when it happened, but the towing charge and other costs were quite high. I thank my lucky stars because just two days before, I had passed a tractor-trailer going 75 mph. This all could have been prevented had I heeded the warning.

**Don't buy a boat** unless you're going to get a lot of enjoyment from it. Most people don't get much use out of a boat, and it can be costly to maintain and repair one. In many areas, boating is seasonal, so you may get to use it for only a limited time each year. And if the weather isn't good, you may not be able to use it during the boating season. You will probably need a trailer and a powerful vehicle to transport the boat. All these expenses add up, and that's not including fuel, registration, and insurance. I read somewhere that BOAT can stand for Break Out Another Thousand, and boats also have a terrible resale value. So, unless you can afford it and you're going to use it a lot, invest the money instead and let it grow. The same advice applies to snowmobiles, four wheelers, and any toys you don't really need or get use from. If you have to have a toy, buy a bicycle; it will be cheaper and can provide you with exercise.

**Do your own home repairs.** Some will be out of your league, but you can do many of them. Remember that you're paying the repair people with after-tax dollars, so depending on your tax bracket, you're actually paying much more for services. Doing your own household repairs can save you a lot of money, and it will give you a sense of accomplishment. Most of the time, you'll find a YouTube video that can teach you how to make the repair. Big jobs may have to be hired out, but if you know a little about home repair and understand the costs of materials, you're in a better position not to overpay for the service.

**Do your own investing.** You don't have to be a financial genius to invest your money. You're most likely paying high fees for something you could do yourself. A little education in this area can go a long way. Most financial advisers cannot predict what the markets will do any better than you can. You're essentially paying them a hefty fee for reassurance and pseudo-confidence. A 1 or 2 percent fee can really diminish your returns if paid over many years. Just reading a couple of investment books can really help. People can do quite well investing in index funds and holding onto them for decades. If you have no interest in doing your own financial planning, find a fee-for-service planner and only pay for the work that is done. Or you may want to consider one of the computer programs now available. These programs can help you determine what to invest in and when to rebalance your portfolio.

**If you're capable, you may want to do your own taxes.** There are several computer programs that can walk you through it. You can also learn how to write your will or start a simple trust. You can then invest the money that would have paid for these services.

**Don't loan money you can't afford to lose.** It's unlikely you'll be paid back when you lend money, so view it as a gift. If you do get paid back, be thankful. It's best not to loan money to friends or relatives because, in most cases, you won't get your money back and the relationship will sour. If you want to lend the money, do so, but don't get upset when you're not paid back. The times I loaned out money, I never got paid back, but I kept that possibility in mind and didn't let it upset me when it happened.

On the same note, never co-sign a loan for someone. Doing so has big potential for loss because if the person doesn't make the payments, you're on the hook. It may seem like the nice thing to do at first, but you'll feel a lot different if you're paying for something you're not getting any use from. A female relative of mine co-signed a loan for a car. The primary person stopped making payments and left the state. My relative had to make the payments while the primary party was using the car. She ended up paying for the car, and after a legal battle, she got the automobile, but by that time, it was practically worthless. Think before you sign.

**Avoid any unlawful behaviors.** If you're dishonest or unscrupulous in your dealings with people, you'll pay the price, not only fiscally, but emotionally and mentally. The consequences of dishonest actions will weigh you down. You'll tarnish your reputation and lose the respect of friends and family. We all know that bad things can happen to good people, but if we do something negative that we could have controlled or prevented, it's much more difficult to deal with. Becoming involved in a lawsuit prior to or during retirement can drastically lower your self-esteem (and bank account). Always be cognizant of the consequences of your actions.

**Don't get a pet unless you can truly afford to own one.** This one may sound heartless, but pets can be expensive and put a dent in your savings. Not only is the cost of feeding most pets high, but vet bills, insurance, and kennel costs can really add up. If your pet injures someone or damages property, you could be paying out a lot of money. I remember once talking to a grocery store worker during the Christmas season. Her dog needed emergency surgery because of a ruptured intestine. She was a single college student struggling to meet expenses with a part-time job. The vet bill was over $1,000, and needless to say, her holiday season was affected.

That's what got me thinking that it's probably best to wait to get a pet until you can afford one, in both time and money. Once you can afford to support the pet, by all means get one. They can add a lot of enjoyment to your life when the time is right.

**Retire the television.** Most of what you see on TV has very little usefulness. The news is repetitive and depressing. In fact, I could have included TV earlier when I spoke about eliminating toxicity from your life. We can be exposed to a lot of violence and the mistreatment of people by watching TV. The reality shows are bizarre and getting worse. Don't we have enough of our own reality? What TV portrays is skewed and misleading. It's all for entertainment and doesn't do anything to enhance our lives. It is about what sells—not what would be beneficial to our lives. Cutting off the cable will save you a ton of money over the years, and you'll be less apt to fall prey to TV ads.

I've been without cable TV for seventeen years, and I don't miss it. I keep up with the news on the Internet and by reading the paper. Television can have some benefit if you watch educational shows and limit its use. But, in general, watching a lot of TV also takes you away from other activities that are healthier, like exercise and mind expansion.

**Don't get ticketed.** Americans love to go to games and sporting events. We all know this can be quite expensive. By the time you add up the cost of tickets, food and drink, parking, gas, and, sometimes, lodging, you've spent a small fortune. The players have all the fun, and you get the tab, traffic jams, and annoying fans. There is always another game and the seasons never seem to end. Can you even remember who won the game a month later? If you must go to sporting events, at least limit them, or better yet, go to a high school game for a fraction of the cost. The fans can be just as obnoxious and the game just as exciting. The parking spots are easier to get into and so are the bathrooms. When the big game is unavoidable, buy your ticket in advance. Don't get scalped.

**Don't go into debt.** Debt is prison, especially during retirement. Your time and money will not be your own until the debt is paid. There will always be that lurking feeling that you owe money to someone. If you have no choice about going into debt, try to pay it off as soon as you're able. Be careful not to accumulate credit card debt; pay cash for purchases or pay off your credit card balance every month. You lose the ability to save money if you're spending it on interest payments on loans.

**Avoid buying flavored drinks and expensive coffees.** These small expenses add up, and they also add to your waistline. The best drink for you is water, and it's relatively inexpensive (nearly free, if you get it out of the tap). If you want to drink those special beverages, at least limit the number. If you're spending $3 daily on drinks or coffee, that's $90 a month or $1,095 a year. If each drink is 300 calories, that's 2.57 pounds a month or potentially thirty pounds of extra weight in one year. It would take you at least sixty minutes of daily exercise to burn those 300 calories. It's much easier to gain the weight than to lose it, but you want the gain in your wallet, not your waist. Remember, small leaks can sink big ships, and a continuous drip can wear down a rock.

**Visit restaurants infrequently.** What you pay for one meal could easily buy a week's worth of food. And a lot of restaurant food isn't that good for you, often containing too much salt, sugar, and calories. Eating out should be a special, infrequent event.

**Take good care of any equipment you have.** Conduct the recommended maintenance on your car, lawnmower, snow blower, or any other equipment you've got. It can be costly to replace and repair them if they are not well-maintained.

**Go on less expensive vacations.** Traveling can be a wonderful, life-enhancing experience. But if you're trying to grow your retirement fund, blowing five figures on a vacation can slow down the process. We go on vacation to recharge our batteries, but quite often, we come home exhausted, with a depleted bank account, and a gastrointestinal (GI) upset. Be creative and think up less costly vacations that can be fun and relaxing. You can also save money by traveling during the off-season. Good memories don't have to cost a bundle.

**Pay your bills with a smile.** There is a way that paying certain bills can be less punishing and possibly profitable—the companies you make monthly payments to may be traded on the stock exchanges. If so, you could buy shares in those companies. That way, if the companies do well, you benefit, and if they pay a dividend, that could help defray the amounts you pay to them. This strategy could be applied to phone, cable, and health insurance companies. You could also buy shares in companies that produce frequently purchased items like toothpaste. The money you have been saving needs to go somewhere.

**Make sure you always have adequate insurance.** What type and how much insurance you need is beyond the scope of this book, so check with a trustworthy agent or research it yourself. If you don't have the needed insurance and something happens, you could be wiped out. One trip to the emergency room can cost several thousand dollars. If you are the primary earner, and were to die, would your survivors be able to pay the bills? During your working years, you have a greater chance of becoming disabled and being unable to work than you have of dying. Don't take the chance of being without proper insurance coverage. I saw it all too often, in practice, where people's life savings were decimated by an unexpected event. Once you have enough savings and no debt, you can start paring down on some forms of insurance, like life and disability coverage. If you have an older car, you may want to reduce its coverage also.

**Marry the right person and stay together.** That is, of course, if marriage is in your plans. Divorce can potentially ruin any retirement plan. I am not a marriage counselor or couple's expert, but I would like to share with you some observations and experiences. Choose your marriage partner carefully. If a person treats other people badly, he or she will treat you badly after you are married. If a person uses drugs, drinks excessively, or overspends before marriage, you guessed it, there will be problems after marriage. If you can't be yourself in a relationship, look elsewhere because the act can't last forever. Watch for inconsistencies in their behavior like saying one thing and doing another, or expecting you to act a certain way, but they act just the opposite. Most importantly, before you tie the knot, make sure your future spouse is truly and sincerely able to empathize with you and others. The inability to empathize will have negative effects on you and your future children. Books are available to help determine whether this an issue, in your relationship. *The Human Magnet Syndrome* by Ross Rosenberg is an excellent read about how to recognize personality traits in people who can't empathize and why we attract them. If you are married and a split up is unavoidable, at least work on how to divide the money fairly; otherwise, it all may go to the attorneys.

These are just a few of the ways you can save money for retirement. It's also important to let your family know about your financial retirement goals. If you share your views with them, they may be more cooperative and spend less money.

Some people don't want to save. They want to enjoy their money while they can. This is an okay attitude if you don't think you're going to live to retirement age, but the odds are that you will. One of the major financial regrets of older people is that they didn't start saving earlier. You don't have to save everything, but start to save as much as you can without feeling deprived. Once you get in the habit, it gets easier.

In retirement, you're looking for financial freedom. You want to have income from your investments that will cover your living expenses. It will take time to accumulate this income, but with effort, the timeframe can be reduced. Once you have financial freedom, you're not dependent on anyone for money. You can continue to work, but you don't have to. You can direct your life as you want. Doesn't that sound better than living beyond your means? You get to call the shots. If you're not satisfied with your current work situation, you can leave and do something else. Innumerable possibilities exist when you don't need to have a job to support yourself. We can't depend on the government to support us in retirement, and our kids probably won't enjoy keeping us afloat (if they even have the means). In some circumstances, we may need to depend on the government or family, but we should make every effort to avoid it.

Invest any bonuses or any money that is paid to you unexpectedly. This is most likely money you don't need to live on, so why not invest it and allow it to grow? Most people would spend the money as soon as they get it, but by doing that, you lose its growth potential. Consider spending a percentage of it, if that would make you feel better, but invest the bulk of it. There are many other ways you can save money before and during retirement, but you don't need to save every cent. The expenses you have and the amount of money you need during retirement will depend on the type of lifestyle you want. That lifestyle will be different for everyone. I have found that I can live on far less and still do everything I want.

As we already know, life can throw us some curveballs, and it is possible we could lose all or a portion of our money during retirement. If you or I could predict the future, we could save only the amount we need and be totally prepared. We know this is not possible, so it is better to over-save and be prepared. Therefore, we don't want to live beyond our means. Out-living your money could affect your wellbeing. Do you want to be financially free, or do you want the service people and sales representatives to be emancipated? The ability to finance your own life frees you to do what you want and to grow in areas that tickle your fancy. But not too fancy if you are trying to save. What do you do when you have enough money from investments coming in to cover your expenses? The principle that is generating the income must be preserved, but you can spend some or most of this income. The percentage that you would be able to spend and not be affected by inflation would need to be determined. The best that life has to offer is in the form of experiences and enjoying the fruits of our labor. Once you have enough money to meet your needs, by all means have fun.

Remember that living the being RETIRED philosophy, increasing your self-esteem, putting a positive spin on things, getting rid of negativity, optimizing your health, and being on solid financial ground leads to positive growth. This positive growth relieves PMS, which allows further positive growth, and the cycle continues. By instituting these practices, your attitude is continuing to climb at double-warp speed.

## Questions for Reflection

1) How can you reduce expenses?

2) Are you using all the stuff that you have?

3) Are there memberships that you are paying dues for but no longer use?

4) Could you live without TV?

5) What are the fees for the financial advice you are getting?

6) Do you have enough and the right types of insurance?

Chapter Ten
# Engage in Lifelong Activity and Learning

WHEN I FIRST retired, I missed the challenges of work. I didn't feel like I was making good use of my mind. This happens because our minds need to be challenged. When we first retire, we may feel irrelevant and useless because we aren't using our problem-solving abilities. We can feel that the challenges we face, after retirement, are mundane or unimportant and not worth putting any time into. Our knowledge, skills, and experience may seem no longer needed or out-of-date. This may be true in terms of your old occupation. Maybe those abilities will never be needed again, or you won't find anything as challenging as your previous jobs. You may not fit with the current corporate culture but don't feel ready for the non-working culture. It can be very demoralizing and frustrating to put so much time and energy into a career, only to feel disconnected in the end.

But at this stage in your life, you have nothing to prove. I'm sure you could keep up to speed if you really wanted to, but hopefully, you have the desire to move on to new things. You may have lost a step or two, and maybe you can't do the job like you did before, but now you don't have to, and why would you want to? If you're alive, you have value. If you're living life successfully and happily, you're serving as an example and inspiration to others. There are many ways to challenge your mind in retirement; it is just up to you to discover how. If you're continuing to develop yourself in positive ways, you're less apt to feel irrelevant. Remember that this feeling is in your mind. Your new challenge can be to find new challenges. Put your mind to use by searching for activities you are interested in and that will pose problems to solve.

These activities can be unique and tailored to your individual needs. Just like in nature, if we are not busy growing, in some way, we are busy dying. This growth doesn't mean physical. It means growing intellectually, mentally, emotionally, or spiritually. This growth occurs from experiences, working through problems, and study.

Retirement is a gift that will eventually end. That fact makes it all the more important that you enjoy it while you have it. It's the last chance you have at approaching authenticity. You don't have to impress anyone. You can decline events and things you really don't want to do. You can learn about yourself and what you want out of life. This is your time, and when you find something that you're passionate about, you can be involved in it as much as you want.

It may take some work to determine your areas of interest and ability, but the result can be enlightening. Once these areas are discovered and developed, they can add greatly to your enjoyment of retirement. When you discover something you truly enjoy doing, your attitude will change for the better. When you've developed one or more of your natural gifts, you can then begin sharing them with humanity.

Sharing your gifts will improve your retirement and contribute to society. Contributing to society can, in turn, improve your attitude, so it's a continuous and positive cycle. This self-discovery process will not happen overnight. It takes time and effort to discover your natural gifts. Don't try to rush it; take your time and work it through. The detective work can be enjoyable and challenging, but the rewards invaluable.

Start thinking about what you did as a child that you really enjoyed and seemed to have a natural inclination for; then go on from there. Try different activities, or join organizations that interest you and see what develops. Take courses to expand your knowledge in areas of interest. The sky is the limit, but your growth will not happen without your effort. Be patient. Start by devoting a small amount of time every day to this internal work. These small steps will eventually add up.

You used many skills during your working years. You had to be disciplined, motivated, and willing to stick to a task. Those same skills can now be applied to your retirement years. Use your imagination and creative abilities to create the very best retirement possible. Start approaching things with a beginner's mind. When you first started working, you weren't super-proficient at your job, so don't expect to be great at everything you try. Try to find something to get passionate about. It doesn't need to be anything grand or something that will get you recognition. It could be something as simple as spending time with your family or embarking on a path of self-discovery. The greatest thing you can do is learn about yourself. Not in a selfish way, but to find true understanding.

When you're retired, your life may not be as dynamic as it once was, but nor does it have to be. Nobody is dynamic in all aspects of his or her life. When I first retired, I felt like I was going to lose my medical skills, and that if I wanted to go back to work, I would be out of touch. But I discovered so many opportunities for learning that I don't give much thought to lost skills.

### Add Value to Your Life

You can add value in so many areas of your life. Value could be as simple as saying thank you to someone or smiling and saying hello to people you encounter. Perhaps it means showing empathy to a person in need. You can add value to this world by the little things you do. If you're growing in positive ways, you're adding value to yourself and society. Being down and feeling poorly about yourself adds no value, and it is contagious; it can cause other people to avoid you. I'm sure you can remember that when your mother or father was in a bad mood, everyone in the family was irritable. Happiness and joy, which seem to be so rare nowadays, are also contagious. What better service can you provide to society and the world than to spread happiness and joy through your actions and good deeds?

There's a lot that we can be down about in the world. But to wallow in depression because you're no longer needed in the old job market is a complete waste of time. You're not the first person to retire, and you won't be the last. Feeling irrelevant is a state of mind you choose to have.

### Become Creative and Keep Learning

Work on becoming more creative and keep learning. Volunteering, which we'll discuss later, can help you feel useful and keep you learning new things. Lifelong learning can change your mindset and make all the difference in the world to you by increasing your enjoyment of life.

What could be more important than bringing increased joy into your life or another person's life?

After many years of working in the same occupation, you've become proficient at being able to do the job well. You're very competent, and people look to you for guidance and knowledge. This is certainly a great feeling, and most of us like it a lot. When we're good at something, we like it even more. Positive reinforcement strokes the ego and keeps us attached to the job. But what happens when we retire and aren't good at anything else? It's not comfortable and it causes anxiety. If we haven't cultivated other activities, we'll be beginners at anything new we try. Most of the interests we take up after retirement will be new and challenging. We may not be used to being a beginner again, and we may feel embarrassed when people see that we're less than skilled. We may see young children who are more knowledgeable about some activities than we are. This is very hard to accept, and it is one of the reasons why older retired people don't attempt new activities and interests.

It's understandable to feel this way, but it's very limiting. We're all beginners at something, and we can all learn from each other. If you really want to learn something new, you'll have to accept that you won't be the best, at least in the beginning. Learn to swallow your pride and do it anyway. Think about all the new things you might be avoiding because you don't want to appear like a fool. This feeling will have to be curtailed if you're going to make the most of your retirement. So, don't be afraid to try something new to see whether you'll enjoy it. Give it at least six months to see whether your interest as well as your competency improves. If after six months you don't really like it, move on to something else.

### How to Enjoy Being a Beginner

Approach learning something new as an experience and a process, rather than setting a goal of being good at the activity. The process of learning something new is just as rewarding as attaining competence. You may have to temper your goals and become realistic about your ability to obtain your objective; after all, you probably aren't going to become a rock star if you start playing guitar in your sixties. Nor are you going to become a professional golfer if you first play the sport in retirement. But that doesn't mean you can't greatly enjoy these activities.

I have to admit that this beginner mindset has been a problem for me. I've never liked feeling incompetent in anything, even when I was younger. I've loosened up quite a bit over the last couple of years, and I've realized that's the only way to be in retirement.

If you're trying to learn a new skill from someone who is hypercritical, you may give up in frustration. Seek out understanding people who love to teach others, especially the more mature pupils. Doing so will increase your chances for success. By going out on a limb and leaving your comfort zone, many new doors can open up socially. A new interest gives you something to talk about at social events and the chance to meet like-minded people. Just do it!

Since I've retired, I've been playing blues harmonica, and I even attended a harmonica jam camp where I had to get up on stage and play. It was intimidating but fun. Sometimes when I am practicing, I imagine I am in a blues band playing in front of a large audience, and when I finish, the crowd goes wild. I've also started ice fishing and have really learned to enjoy it. Yes, ice fishing can be fun, but you have to dress in the proper attire and the fish have to be hungry. I tried bridge, but I didn't enjoy it as much as physical activity. Try new things, and if they don't work out, try something else. Get to know a variety of people and learn what they are doing. It is a great way to get exposure to other areas of potential interest.

Being a beginner is like getting a second chance at childhood. If you had a good childhood, you get to do it again, and if your childhood wasn't so good, you can give it another go. Don't take yourself and your lack of ability too seriously. Notice I've been talking of competency, not perfectionism. You may never be able to perform to your liking, but that's no excuse not to try.

When you have a problem trying a new activity, think of ways you can make it more interesting and possibly fun. Use your imagination to come up with things that are fun to do. Try to think like a kid again, and start doing what you find to be fun.

Start by becoming curious about new activities available to you. There are innumerable things you can do or learn about. If you find something you're interested in and take a class or workshop, not only can you learn more about the subject, but you can also meet people with similar interests.

### Explore Artistic and Creative Pursuits

We waste a lot of time and energy living in the past. Living in the present frees up a lot of time and energy that can be used to explore and enjoy our creativity. We each have unique talents, interests, and abilities. Some of these gifts are not even known to us and some are underdeveloped. You now have the time and energy to grow in areas you may have overlooked in the past.

Learning some form of art is a great way to prepare for retirement. If you haven't had the opportunity to experience your artistic ability, retirement can be a great time to discover it. Developing your creativity can be a great means of self-expression and also a lot of fun. These types of activities are done for the joy of doing them. You don't have to make a living doing them, so the pressure is off. At the same time, becoming competent at the new art form can build your confidence and self-esteem. At least initially, you may have to deal with criticism, both from yourself and others, but working on artistic, creative projects also helps develop patience. You can't rush good art. It's a great way to get into the flow or the present moment. There are numerous art forms to choose from; find one that interests you. For example, as I mentioned, I find playing the harmonica interesting and relaxing.

We all know that the better we are at something, the more we enjoy doing it. If possible, explore new activities long before you retire. If you play an instrument, keep playing it after you retire. If you paint or write, keep at it. It's never too late to learn, but it's easier to keep doing something you already enjoy and know how to do. The happiest people seem to be the ones expressing themselves through some form of art.

It's also important to incorporate play and fun into your life. Sometimes we forget that we need play in our lives. Life can be much too serious; it may be full of obligations and commitments that occupy most or all of your free time. When that happens, we lose the capacity to lighten things up and have fun. Too much seriousness can lead to a skewed view of life. If life is approached as if it's a game and we're merely players in that game, then we don't take things as seriously.

Getting involved in some sort of sport can be an excellent way of having fun. It can also relieve stress and help you sleep better. You may be better able to handle some hassles in your life by releasing pent up emotions on the court or playing field. Overall, it's a good thing to do given that it can benefit you in many ways.

## Wean Yourself Off Social Media

Start weaning yourself off of social media or significantly reducing the time you're glued to the Internet. It's a waste of your time and energy. Sometimes it can lead to anger, jealousy, and melancholy feelings. A small amount of time on the Internet is probably all right, but it should be limited.

You should also pay attention to how you feel after you've visited certain websites. If negative feelings result, those sites should be avoided. Spending too much time on social media takes you away from more beneficial activities. Instead, you could be developing a hobby, exercising, or getting out into nature. You could be relaxing or reflecting on your life. Social media can be so habit-forming that some people may check their phones hundreds of times a day. Some are checking for messages while at work or driving. These behaviors can lead to very bad outcomes. Do yourself a favor and wean yourself off of your electronic devices. The Internet can provide the opportunity to take courses, listen to lectures, and read about areas of interest, but just surfing the net can be a waste of time. Use your computer properly and only in ways that will enhance your life.

## Learn from Other People's Experiences

Start becoming more open-minded about learning from other people's experiences. We can learn something from everyone. Some people have gone through life-changing experiences, so it can be life-enhancing to get to know these kinds of people and tap into their knowledge. They may share insights that you can benefit from.

I especially admire and respect people who are recovering from addictions. These people have lived through hell and landed on their feet. They certainly understand what's important in life and how to live better.

Learning from people who have survived a life-threatening illness can help us to set priorities and put our problems in perspective. Reading about people who have overcome great obstacles can be awe-in-spiring. Older people are rich in knowledge and experience. Unfortunately, this knowledge is not often welcomed or appreciated.

When we're younger, we think we know it all and have nothing of value to learn from the elderly. Granted, many older people have not adjusted well and are very cynical, but you can still learn something from them—even if it's realizing that you don't want to be like them. You can do things differently to avoid the same fate. Most older people have had to overcome obstacles and adjust to setbacks in their lives. Why not see these people as an invaluable resource? Older people are often eager to share their knowledge and experiences; all you've got to do is ask. Most of what they've lived through you'll be going through at a future time. Ask them what they would do over if they could. Ask them about what regrets they may have. What do they think is important for happiness? Sometimes their answers will be clichéd or not very helpful, but sometimes they will bring up something that will resonate with you. You have to be a miner looking for nuggets of gold. You may have to sift through a lot of dirt to find something of benefit. But when you do, it's truly worth it and the interaction can be very enjoyable and beneficial for both of you.

When I was in practice and had the time, I would ask patients all kinds of questions, especially those patients who appeared to be thriving. I swear that I learned more from them than they learned from me.

Start taking an interest in people. Find out what they're doing right and incorporate it into your life. You don't need to reinvent the wheel. When soldiers go to boot camp, they're taught skills that were learned by other soldiers many years before. If their training always had to be reinvented, nothing would have ever evolved or improved. When we develop a sincere interest in others, not only can we learn something, but we direct our attention away from ourselves. We become less self-centered, and that makes life more fun.

You have to be open to this type of interaction, be willing to hear another's point of view, and be able to accept what he or she says as a potential learning tool. Without guidance from our parents and teachers, we would be lost. You still have the final say about what you choose to incorporate into your life. When I was a kid, I can still remember my uncle, who was a smoker at the time, telling me, "If I ever catch you smoking, I'll beat the &%#$ out of you." Needless to say, I took this as advice and never smoked. I thought about that interchange and didn't give in to peer pressure.

Life is very short, and we only live it once, so nobody can know everything, but by being open to others' knowledge and wisdom, we may be able to circumvent some of life's sufferings.

Self-help books can be a great source of knowledge. Most are written by people who have struggled with and overcome the problem they're writing about. There's a self-help book for almost every problem we might encounter. If you have a problem, most likely someone else has had to deal with the same thing. Would you rather learn from someone who has experienced something firsthand, or someone who has lived it vicariously?

Knowledge is power, but you must also put it into action. All the advice and recommendations we get are useless unless we utilize that knowledge so it will benefit us in some way.

### Try Volunteering

Doing things for others is built into our genetics. We all believe we can contribute to society or to a cause. Volunteering can be a great way to benefit society and ourselves. It makes us feel good when we help others. Now is a good time to hone in on the areas that really interest you and where you would like to have more involvement. If you haven't thought about it too much before, now is the time to look around to see whether something piques your interest. Try several volunteer opportunities to see which one might be the best fit once you're retired. Volunteering is also a good way to meet other people. The volunteer options are endless, so limit your involvement to those causes you feel passionate about and eliminate the ones you don't feel excited about.

Volunteer situations can also have a hierarchy and politics, just like work. If you volunteer for a board or committee, there may also be some potential liability. So before joining a volunteer situation, give it some thought and only get involved with the ones you really feel passionate about.

At the same time, volunteering may not be good if it becomes an obligation. If we become dependent on it for our happiness, we'll suffer when it's gone. It's better to get your internal house in order before working on the external parts. Most people volunteer with the idea that it will make them feel better. This may be true, but they may feel worse if it's not the right fit. We don't want to do something just to occupy our time. It is better to find something we feel very strongly about, we enjoy, and that will make a difference in society.

### *Never Stop Learning*

Begin to develop a lifelong aptitude for learning. Learning new things can be fun and personally beneficial. You could learn how to write your own will or do your own estate planning. Or you could learn more about investing your money and doing it yourself instead of paying someone to do it. Or you could start doing your own taxes now that you have the time. You can get personal satisfaction and save money if you do some of your home maintenance.

Learning new things is the key to a happy life. Once we stop learning, we start to deteriorate mentally. A lifelong learning philosophy will help you maintain a positive attitude. It may be an interest that you didn't have time to pursue before retirement, or it may be learning how to adapt to a new situation in life, like technology. Curiosity keeps us learning. Every experience is a chance for us to learn something new.

Many people aren't interested in learning when their formal education stops. That is unfortunate because continuing to learn new things certainly makes life more enjoyable. There is so much to learn and get excited about. I have a keen interest in the mind and body and how they interact. Since retiring, I've been able to read several books on this subject. I also have learned a little about music and playing an instrument. Not only are these topics interesting, but they're also fun. I haven't been to a social gathering without having a great conversation with someone who loves to play an instrument.

My wife likes to garden, so she has taken courses on how to grow plants more efficiently. She's also learning how to make jewelry, and she always has a keen eye out for new recipes. If you live close to a university, you can take courses for credit or just audit them.

Learning about investing and money management can be enjoyable and money-saving. I do all my own investing and financial management. It's not that hard. I took the coursework and have a certificate in financial planning; in fact, the most beneficial thing I learned about

financial planners is that you don't need one. Unlike other professionals like doctors or dentists, you can do the work yourself. With a little
knowledge and investment firms like Schwab, Fidelity, and Vanguard,
you can do just as well and, most of the time, better than an advisor.
Remember that their fees can really add up and decrease your potential income.

It's important that you have an interest in your finances because no
one will care more about your resources than you. Advisors get paid
whether you make or lose money. In most cases, very little time is required for money management. If you think your manager is looking
at your account daily or even monthly, you're most likely mistaken.
The money you save could be used for *your* pleasure, not that of your
money manager.

I've taken several online courses and learned a lot; they were far
less pressure than taking a traditional college course. I signed up for
Amazon's Kindle Unlimited—for a monthly fee you can read an unlimited number of ebooks. Not every book is available and not all of the
authors are well-known, but I've learned many new things on various
subjects. When I was having trouble selling my house, I downloaded a
couple of books on that subject and found several good suggestions. I
implemented them, which I believe helped me sell the house.

### Develop Social Outlets Plus the Ability to Be Alone

We have addressed this topic before, but it is worth repeating. It's
not good to isolate ourselves from society. When we're retired, it can
seem like everyone has places to go and people to be with, while we're
no longer part of the rest of the world. Other people have their rou-
tines and activities, but our days are open-ended and unplanned. I can
remember thinking that I no longer fit—society had moved ahead and
I was left behind.

That's why it's good to have social outlets and people in our lives.
If we don't make that effort, we can become more and more estranged
from humanity. The more we avoid interactions with people, the less
people will want to socialize with us. Your wellbeing will be helped by
having a few friends you can do things with and commiserate with. You
don't need a dozen friends—just a couple of close ones will be invaluable. It can take time to find and develop these kinds of relationships,

but they are well worth the effort and time. As they say, "It is better to have two fifty cent pieces than a hundred pennies." The same applies to friends. If you do interesting activities, others will be interested in you.

It's also important to learn to be happy and content when you're alone. Enjoying your own company is a tremendous asset in being able to make the most of your life. If we can be secure in our solitude and develop the ability to entertain ourselves, we'll always be content, even if we have to spend time alone. So, learn not only to tolerate being alone, but to thrive on it.

As with most things in life, there's a healthy balance to strike. It's not good to spend all your time alone, and it's not good to spend no time alone. I've always enjoyed my alone time. I don't have a problem with entertaining myself or going places by myself. But the idea of spending all my time alone doesn't interest me at all. I enjoy the social circles I'm part of. Start developing your own social circle if you don't already have one because the benefits will be many.

### *Develop an Exercise Routine*

Aging is a big problem for most of us. We don't like getting older. The cosmetic industry is proof of that. I honestly thought I could outrun the aging process. Even though I was a doctor who practiced geriatrics for many years, who saw the reality of aging and mortality up close, I didn't believe the same aging problems would happen to me. (Talk about wishful thinking!)

Today, I exercise nearly every day for at least an hour. I also do strength training several days a week. This gives me the continued ability to do most of the things I enjoy doing. It's so important that we take care of ourselves through exercise and diet. There are no guarantees that taking extra care of yourself will help you live longer, but the odds are it will. Exercise will allow you to enjoy your life more. It's a great way to add structure to your life, and it has been shown to reduce the symptoms of depression.

Facing the reality of aging has been a difficult undertaking, but I'm learning to accept it. I don't have the stamina and strength I used to, and I can't stay up as long as I could years ago. When I weight train, I don't recover as quickly as in the past. But I'm very grateful for the abilities I still have, and I try to maintain them.

I hope by now you realize that doing retirement right is an active process. It is your new occupation and you get to be the boss. You now have the tools to develop and implement a great retirement life. No matter what your health is or what your experiences have been, you can still enjoy the rest of your life. Most of the things we have been striving for just aren't that important at this stage in life. The best thing a person can do is strive to be him- or herself. As Socrates said, "The unexamined life is not worth living."

Life can seem long and depressing if we let it. Getting involved with life and really living the experiences makes it appear short but enjoyable. When I was a kid, being in church seemed like an unending hour because I would just watch the clock and not participate. Now when I go to church and sing and pay attention to the readings, the time goes by in a flash. If you are participating and enjoying the process of your life, it will seem very short. On the other hand, life can seem long and meaningless if you are not actively involved.

During this retirement process, I have learned a lot about myself and what I feel is important. Old beliefs and values are hard to change, but change they must if we are going to thrive when retired. Some of the old beliefs are not of any use, and some can cause great discomfort when we retire. Hanging on to worn-out beliefs is like moving from Alaska to Arizona and never removing your parka.

Everything in this book has been used by me to enhance my retirement, and it can be utilized by you to do the same. None of this advice is magical; it can be applied by everyone. These suggestions will stand the test of time; they are simple in concept and cost nothing monetarily, but effort is needed. They are common sense, but we all know how much common sense can be ignored.

There is so much that I didn't realize about retirement and later life issues. I didn't comprehend the magnitude of the effect retirement can have on a person's self-esteem and the importance of letting go of the negativity we may be carrying forward. An analogy would be bringing all the baggage from a divorce into your new marriage.

I felt the need to write this book because I sensed that a lot of people struggle with this big change in life. It's not easy to give up something we've identified with and that may be the only thing people have known us for. It can make us feel invisible. But believe me, this can be the best time of your life—you just have to work out the bumps.

The feelings you are having about missing work, any work, are only in your mind. I had to learn this for myself, and I searched for answers through study and self-reflection. The books I read appeared to be lacking some key ingredients to a happier retirement. Since I put the practices I've shared in this book into motion, my attitude has improved exponentially. Getting to know myself better has made all the difference in the world. I now better understand some of my behaviors and how to live a more authentic life. As the saying goes, "If you can't find the book you want to read, write it." That is what compelled me to write this book.

Realize that if you are struggling with the changes brought about by retirement, you are not alone, and with effort and time, things will get better.

### *Benjamin Franklin: The Model Retiree*

After writing this book, I wanted to find someone who was a well-known or historical figure I could use as an example of someone who had lived by the concepts laid out in this book. Ultimately, Benjamin Franklin came to mind. He retired from printing in his forties, and after retiring, he went on to invent many things and continued to learn. During his retirement, he was a scientist, diplomat, inventor, musician, writer, and exercise enthusiast. He most likely practiced the recommendations found in this book, albeit they were not available yet in print. His self-esteem was certainly high, and he adhered to a positive lifestyle. He limited his alcohol consumption and drank mostly water. He also professed frugality and lived well into his eighties, which was quite remarkable for that time period. His never-ending curiosity helped him have an inspiring life. His greatest contributions to humanity were after he retired; he continued to invent and discover things throughout his life. Of course, he was not perfect, but most would agree that he had an extraordinary life. We may never achieve the kinds of accomplishments he did, but we can still fill our lives with interesting things.

Here are a few words of wisdom from Benjamin Franklin that you can apply to your retirement.

### Financial

"Early to bed and early to rise, makes a man healthy, wealthy, and wise."

"A penny saved is a penny earned."

"An investment in knowledge always pays the best interest."

"He that is of the opinion money will do everything may well be suspected of doing everything for money."

"Rather go to bed without dinner than to rise in debt."

### Health

"Eat to live; live not to eat."

"A full belly makes a bad brain."

"To lengthen thy life, lessen thy meals."

### Time

"Never leave that till tomorrow which you can do today."

"By failing to prepare, you are preparing to fail."

"You delay, but time will not."

"Time lost is never found again."

Remember that living the being RETIRED philosophy, improving your self-esteem, putting a positive spin on things, getting rid of negativity, optimizing your health, keeping a solid financial situation, and pursuing lifelong learning leads to positive growth. This positive growth cures PMS, which allows further positive growth, and the cycle continues. Following these practices will keep your attitude in the stratosphere. If you develop this aptitude and do these practices, your attitude will never lose altitude.

Good luck and I wish you all the best.

"Live as if you were to die tomorrow. Learn as if you were to live forever."
— *Mahatma Gandhi*

# WARNING!

I F YOU DECIDE to seek medical attention for Post-Work Melancholy
Syndrome, only refer to it as such. Using the abbreviated version
(PMS) may result in funny looks, chuckles, smirks, and possibly inap-
propriate and harmful medical treatment.

### *Questions for Reflection*

1) What activities inspire you?

2) What do you enjoy reading about?

3) Who do you look up to and what activities are they involved in?

4) Is there an art that you practiced in the past and could get back
   to doing?

5) What do you want to learn more about?

6) What would you tell a friend to do to enhance his/her retirement?

℞

# Resources

## *Financial Books*

*The Millionaire Next Door: The Surprising Secrets of America's Wealthy* by Thomas J. Stanley and William D. Danko

*Your Money or Your Life* by Vicki Robin and Joe Dominquez

*The Total Money Makeover: Classic Edition: A Proven Plan for Financial Fitness* by Dave Ramsey

*The Millionaire in You* by Michael LeBoeuf, PhD

*The Only Investment Guide You Will Ever Need* by Andrew Tobias

*The Richest Man in Babylon* by George S. Clason

The Book of Ecclesiastes in the Bible

## *Retirement Books*

*How to Retire Happy, Wild and Free: Retirement Wisdom That You Won't Get from Your Financial Advisors* by Ernie Zelinski

*The Retirement Maze: What You Should Know Before and After You Retire* by Rob Pascale and Louis Primavera

*The Psychology of Retirement: Coping With the Transition from Work* by Derek Mine

*The Top Five Regrets of the Dying* by Bronnie Ware

*Happy Retirement: The Psychology of Reinvention* by Megan Kaye and Kenneth S. Schultz

## Books on the Mind
*As a Man Thinketh* by James Allen
*The Strangest Secret* by Earl Nightingale
*The Six Pillars of Self-Esteem* by Nathaniel Branden

## Harmonica Books
*Rock n' Blues Harmonica* by Jon Gindick

## Internet Blogs
A Satisfying Retirement: https://satisfyingretirement.blogspot.com/
Kathy's Retirement Blog: https://kathysretirementblog.com/

R̶X

## About the Author

D̲R. BASH GREW up in a rural community in the Upper Peninsula of Michigan. Growing up the son of a family physician, he experienced his father's office being located in their home. This gave him exposure to the medical field from an early age. In 1983, he received his medical degree and completed a family practice residency. He completed a Master's in Public Health degree with a concentration in occupational medicine in 2001. He also has a certificate in financial planning and retirement coaching.

Dr. Bash practiced family and geriatric medicine in rural Lower Michigan for twenty-five years. He has a keen interest in the connection between the mind and body. His Master's project was on how workplace stress affects workers.

After a slow start with retirement, Dr. Bash now knows that with the right attitude, it can be the best time of a person's life. Dr. Bash has been retired for over five years and lives in the Upper Peninsula with his wife, daughter, and cat. He enjoys skiing, fishing, reading, hiking, and learning to play harmonica.